Why FISH PISS MATTERS

Why FISH PISS MATTERS

ON THE LAST AUTHENTIC BOHEMIA

Andy Brown

Véhicule Press

Published with the generous assistance of the Canada Council for the Arts, the Canada Book Fund of the Department of Canadian Heritage, and the Société de développement des entreprises culturelles du Québec (SODEC).

Canada

SODEC Québec

Canada Council for the Arts Conseil des arts du Canada

Original cover design by Caro Caron
Cover adapted by David Drummond
Set in Minion and Bodoni by Simon Garamond

Dépôt légal, Library and Archives Canada and the Bibliothèque nationale du Québec, second trimester 2025

Library and Archives Canada Cataloguing in Publication
Title: Why Fish piss matters : on the last authentic bohemia / Andy Brown.
Names: Brown, Andrew George, 1968- author Description: Includes index.
Identifiers: Canadiana (print) 20250170140 | Canadiana (ebook) 20250173638 | ISBN 9781550656862 (softcover) | ISBN 9781550656893 (EPUB)
Subjects: LCSH: Fish piss. | LCSH: Subculture—History. | LCSH: Bohemianism—History. | LCSH: Fan magazines—Social aspects—Québec (Province)—Montréal—History—20th century. | LCSH: Zines—Social aspects—Québec (Province)—Montréal—History—20th century. | LCSH: Underground periodicals—Québec (Province)—Montréal—History—20th century. | LCSH: Comic books, strips, etc.—Québec (Province)—Montréal—History—20th century. | LCSH: Canadian literature—20th century—History and criticism.
Classification: LCC HM646 .B76 2025 | DDC 306/.1—dc23

Published by Véhicule Press, Montréal, Québec, Canada
www.vehiculepress.com

Distribution in Canada by LitDistCo
www.litdistco.ca

Distribution in the US by Independent Publishers Group
www.ipgbook.com

Printed in Canada

CONTENTS

The past sure makes for great wallpaper.

–LOUIS RASTELLI, *A Fine Ending*

Introduction

When I moved my family and small publishing company to Wolfville, Nova Scotia in 2010, I met an Irish immigrant and professor of sociology at the local arts university. By way of awkward introductions, made more difficult because we were both so obviously "from away," I mentioned my twenty years living in the Plateau/Mile End neighbourhood in Montreal. His eyes lit up when he heard this. He asked excitedly about my time there and was genuinely shocked to find me here, in a small town, thousands of miles from that hotbed of cultural activity. He told me, "You make the things that give us academics something to write about."

My background in Montreal obviously meant something to him. I discovered he was a huge fan of the music that came out of Constellation Records, started at the same time, in the same neighbourhood, as my publishing operation, Conundrum Press. He talked like this was somehow important. He felt that this time and place in history, of which I was an insider, genuinely mattered. His enthusiasm got me thinking. *Why* does it matter? In the late 1990s, I was just struggling to get by like everyone else I knew, bulking up on bagels and cheese pizza slices to absorb the beer and save money, trying to write stories in shotgun apartments interrupted by screaming neighbours, freelancing, dodging the circumstances that would bring me to welfare. What was it about the time and place I was such a part of, that shaped who I am today, that mattered to someone who wasn't there?

We were part of an anglophone bohemian community of writers, artists, musicians, and political activists, but I realize now bohemianism is only recognized in hindsight. What the hell is bohemianism anyway? Is that even what was going on?

I would have seen my first issue of the zine *Fish Piss* in 1996 while sunk in a red velvet couch in the brightly painted living room of my huge four-bedroom apartment on Fairmount Ave, for which I was splitting the rent of $600. (If you squint hard enough you can make it out in the 1974 film version of Mordecai Richler's *The Apprenticeship of Duddy Kravitz*). My future roommate, Billy Mavreas, was the cover artist. The yellow cardstock cover was adorned with his highly stylized fish drawing and other than the strange title, the only other text was, *No advertising $1.* I doubt it made a huge impression on me at the time. Billy was heavily involved in the French and English comics communities, and he was always showing me alternative, stapled, crazy, gross, whacked-out publications with names like: *Guillotine, Foetus, Mr Swiz,* or *106U*. Inside, there were some writers I knew from the spoken-word series I attended at Bistro 4, such as Heather O'Neill and Jonathan Goldstein, so maybe I thought it was cool to have comics and spoken-word together. Billy was a community node, straddling the comics, music, and lit types, French and English. I just sat back and absorbed it all.

However, it was not until issue #4 (1998) that I truly took notice of *Fish Piss*. This was for a couple of reasons. The front cover was the first one silkscreened by Simon Bossé, featuring the gorgeous artwork of Jean-Pierre Chansigaud—a very recognizable Plateau balcony in the middle of winter. The back cover was by Marc Bell, who slept on that same red velvet couch on and off over the years. It was larger too, at roughly eighty pages, as opposed to the original 24. The other reason I noticed was because I volunteered to do some of the layout, mostly because Catherine Kidd, my roommate at the time, and myself both had writing in the issue and I wanted to make sure it looked professional. This issue was reviewed in *Broken Pencil* (at the time, called "The Guide to Alternative Culture in Canada"): "What holds it all together, what any real literary venture must have to make the loose ends gel, is a passionate commitment to making things better. That's what Louis does for the mag." *Fish Piss* was becoming representative of many different cultural fields, although I only realize this in hindsight. At the time, I was just along for the ride.

Edited by native Montrealer Louis Rastelli, *Fish Piss* ran for eleven issues from 1996 to 2006 (plus three limited bonus mini-issues). It began as a mash-up of the anglophone spoken-word community and the comics community, both French and English. It featured literary material, comics, essays, interviews with regular folk, politics, and music. Often called Canada's most influential zine, *Fish Piss* arose from the DIY aesthetic of the 1970s punk scene. In fact, editor Rastelli cut his teeth on a Montreal music zine called *RearGarde*, then took over the reins as the editor of *Flaming Poutine*, which transformed into *Fish Piss*. The name riffs off the McLuhan metaphor of how consumers of media affect each other constantly without realizing it, much like fish may not notice that they are swimming in their own urine.

Eventually the publication went from that yellow photocopied zine to a 160-page publication with advertising and worldwide distribution through Tower Records. Being in Montreal, it was bilingual and served to establish a unique "contact zone" of cultural production.

As the reaction of my professor friend proves, the legacy of *Fish Piss* persists, whether due to its role as a time-capsule of 1990s Montreal, or as a window into successful artists' earlier work, or whether the idea of a print publication born of a punk ethos with an open submission policy could influence or even exist in today's internet-saturated corporate-culture. It was the representation of a true bohemian community, and due to the timing, post-Referendum and pre-social media, perhaps the last of its kind. *Fish Piss* is a calling card to a time and place that can be considered Canada's last authentic bohemia.

What's in a Name?

LOUIS RASTELLI WAS BORN in 1969 and raised in Montreal. Both his parents were born in Montreal, almost the entire family on both sides still live in Montreal and have been there since before WWII. He grew up in a bilingual family, or as he describes it, "Despite being in the census as a francophone due to my mom being French, I only ever went to English school and was never really exposed to French-Canadian TV shows or comics or what have you. It's the same as anywhere else in Canada: America was cool, Canada sucked."

At fourteen, while attending conservative Loyola High School in the anglophone neighbourhood of Montreal West, Rastelli was one of a handful of self-described goth-punks. He and his friends snuck into Station Ten and Rising Sun and the original Foufounes Électriques to see local hardcore bands. They passed around mix tapes they made from their purchases at Dutchy's Record Cave.

At fifteen, he discovered local newsprint fanzines filled with record and show reviews, band interviews, and rants. The writing was a revelation to him:

> They were all people like me, from around where I lived, and goddammit if I didn't understand what they wrote better than most anything else I'd ever read. I could tell right away that these people were like me. I'd read them all from cover to cover, and when I read in one called *RearGarde* that they were always looking for new writers, I had to go down there and be a part of this thing myself... Anyone got to write if they were sincere enough about it. It was a very public-oriented thing. Best of all, there was no specific directive controlling the end result. The editors knew that all you needed was an open door, and local people would walk in and represent themselves.

RearGarde, later *EnGuard Quarterly*, ended up with over thirty thousand copies printed and distributed nationally. But with the growth in distribution, it lost touch with the local scene, which was disappointing to Rastelli, who had originally felt part of something larger than himself.

He left town in 1990 to attend the University of Waterloo Architecture School in Kitchener-Waterloo. As he writes many years later in his semi-autobiographical novel *A Fine Ending*, he lived in a huge house with one roommate and tried to make friends: "We had good times there, staying up until four or five every night, recording. Kitchener-Waterloo, to me, felt like a city where you needed to find fun and interesting people to be with because there wasn't much fun and interesting about the town itself.

Cartoonist Marc Ngui was one of the interesting people Rastelli met in Waterloo. When asked what he remembers of Rastelli from that time, Ngui answers:

> I remember him being someone who represented counterculture, turning people on to Zappa and Beefheart and esoteric funk. The student body was a mix of students from various social backgrounds. I was coming from a very safe, mainstream, liberal/working class suburban background, so people like Louis stood out to me. One of my clearest memories of Louis was at an annual student No-Talent competition. I was very shy and terrified of being on stage so did not participate. I remember Louis getting on stage with his guitar and fearlessly strumming through a couple of songs with all his intensity, despite the rowdiness and inattentiveness of the mostly drunken audience… Louis was just about the same human being then as he is now. Creatively adventurous, generous, kind, astute, speaks his mind, empathetic, with a very gentle presence.

According to Ngui, "the school tried to select students who were strong in design, critical comprehension and math and engineering so the student body was made up of many really interesting cross-disciplinary thinkers. I'd categorize Louis as one of those people." It turns out neither Rastelli nor

Ngui ever finished architecture school. After they left, Ngui began to publish his comics in Windsor's *Room* magazine. Rastelli would later use these strips for *Fish Piss*, and the clear line anti-corporate comics would eventually form the base of Ngui, and Conundrum's, first graphic novel, *Enter Avariz* (2002).

Rastelli picked up where he left off after returning to Montreal. "On my first night back in Montreal, I went to a show and ran into the same people I'd seen at all the shows before I left. Most of them had no idea I'd been gone for three years." Rastelli quickly discovered a new zine had emerged called *Flaming Poutine*. It ran five or six issues over a couple of years but was more on the scale Rastelli was comfortable with, just a few hundred copies, photocopied and hand-stapled. But it was enough to start filling the gap again. It was a creative space where recent short works by diverse people came together, reaching a bigger public than any one of them had on their own.

> I immediately started writing for *Flaming Poutine* but then the guy who put it out left town. I complained loudly that it needed to keep going, but no one was really into doing the job. I was given all the material from the last issue that never came out. I found out that the old editor had already collected the money for ads and the advertisers wanted refunds. I decided to change the name for that reason, plus it wasn't a great name. *Fish Piss*

> was one of the title ideas I had, after reading too much McLuhan.

Rastelli explains further:

> It was a metaphor I came up with about the media landscape and how consumers of media affect each other constantly without much realizing it, much like fish may not notice that their own piss is in the water they swim around in. That the initials would remain FP clinched it to have the title be *Fish Piss*.

I wondered if Rastelli was introduced to Marshall McLuhan in his courses at Waterloo. Ngui described the program: "The program at Waterloo was divided into three sections: studio, iconography, and building technology. Iconography was a methodical look at the cultural history of western civilization as a way of teaching students about how culture develops and is influenced and influenced by artistic and philosophic practice." His course in iconography could easily have been part of the spark that began the zine. Rastelli often riffs on the origin of the name in his editorials. In fact, he gives a number of dictionary-style definitions for *Fish Piss* in issue #5:

> Fish Piss
> 1. "What ink was made of, specif. squid urine."
> 2. (euphemism) water i.e. WC Fields: "I don't

drink water—Fish Piss in it." Fish urine is not actually water.
3. (euphemism) writing i.e. "Fish pissing" (also "pissing ink," "ink piss") Spec. writing in a long uninterrupted stream, as if talking to someone.
4. (metaphor) Something you're involved in without noticing it... A mental environment affecting one's feelings without one noticing it.

On the eve of Y2K, Rastelli writes in his editorial (#5, 1999): "Right now, as far as knowing what the media we consume and produce *does*, and what we talk about is *real* or just *perceived as real* because everyone's talking about it like it was, we're no more aware of what we consider to be true than fish are aware of whose piss they happen to swim through." He concludes that "we need to take control of our representation." This is essentially the mandate of the zine.

In his editorial for issue #7, December 2001, just after the 9/11 attacks, he writes how he has been thinking of the "Fish Piss metaphor" and the role of paper and ink in our lives:

> When I buy something at a store, I unwittingly alter the numbers in my bank account. The store owners get a few numbers added to their bank account. And if a marketing firm is tracking the effectiveness of an ad campaign... a number is

> added to a chart showing how their ad campaign is working... then the information could end up changing the look or design of the product I bought.

Such is the metaphor of the fish swimming through its own urine without noticing it. But Rastelli addresses the new reality as well, in which we can't help but notice what is happening around us:

> In a way those in positions of economic and political power depend on us not noticing the cross-relations between reality and paper. I doubt, however, that even they ever imagined such an explosion of both worlds as we all witnessed on September 11, when thousands of sheets of paper referring to odd portions of people's lives were mixed with odd portions of thousands of actual people. This was a true convergence of media and reality... However, for at least a few days there, the paper realm seemed extremely trivial, didn't it?

And in his final editorial in the largest issue #10 he writes: "The title is more than a metaphor, however: many gallons of ink went into printing this issue and though it technically isn't urine, the ink from squid ink sacs is still harvested for use in some quality drawing inks. (Sepia ink, for example, is pure squid ink. I would love to print a whole issue with sepia ink; then you'd *really* be reading fish piss!)"

To make the metaphor personal, a memory comes to mind. I grew up in Vancouver and when I was a teenager, I met my buddy on the beach for his big family reunion one evening. They were visiting from Montreal. At one point his uncle was taking a picture, but in my opinion, he was facing the wrong direction. I turned to him and asked, "Why are you not taking the picture of your family on the beach? What are you taking a picture of?" He looked at me shocked. "Look at the beautiful sunset over the mountains. You don't see that every day." The thing is, I did see it every day. I just didn't notice it because I was always swimming in the natural beauty.

I think the metaphor I like best—and one which sums up my participation in Montreal's bohemian community that included *Fish Piss*, whether it was contributing reviews or layout, going to launches, or lugging heavy machines—is that it was something we were all involved in without noticing it.

What Is a Zine?

The term "zine" encompasses a variety of self-published periodicals and small press publications. They are generally intended for a small audience interested in a particular topic, often considered to be alternative, radical, or fringe and therefore not covered by the mainstream press. Generally, they're created by one person, out of love rather than money. While independent, self-produced printed works have existed since the beginnings of published literature, the term "zine" is specifically derived from science fiction fan literature ("fanzines") commonly thought to date to the 1950s. The rise of punk rock music in the 1970s—with its emphasis on self-produced, unregulated content, distributed largely outside the mainstream music trade—fueled an explosive growth in the publication of zines. While zines may be highly subjective and idiosyncratic and their creators often amateurs, there is an element of community-seeking in their publication.

As Stephen Duncombe writes in his book *Notes from Underground* (1997): "Zines, as physical expressions of their creators, transform representation into presentation." In other words, zine makers don't let mainstream media outlets speak for them; they speak for themselves through their actions, the creating and disseminating of a zine. "In zines, everyday oddballs were speaking plainly about themselves and our society with an honest sincerity, a revealing intimacy, and a healthy 'fuck you' to sanctioned authority—for no money and no recognition, writing for an audience of like-minded misfits."

In *The Book of Zines* (1997) author Chip Rowe defines zines as "tinkertoys for malcontents. They're obsessed with obsession. They're extraordinary and ordinary. They're about strangeness but since it's happening somewhere else, you're kind of relieved. You can get to know people pretty well through their zines, which are always more personal and idiosyncratic than glossy magazines..."

Fredric Wertham was a psychiatrist and cultural critic whose book *The Seduction of the Innocent* (1954) and testimony in Senate subcommittees on juvenile delinquency sparked comic book burnings and the creation of the Comics Code. In 1973, he released the book *The World of Fanzines* which (surprisingly) received good reviews from the creators featured in it. In his book on Wertham, academic Bart Beaty states that:

> Wertham affirmed the value of the urge to create and to communicate with others. Fanzine work, Wertham suggested, was social rather than psychological, and fanzine writers and editors were not alienated from society but rather maintained a deep

desire to communicate and socialize with others who shared similar interests. Given the postwar era consisted of a consumer society, Wertham celebrated the fanzine for its outsider status. He conceptualized this refusal as a form not of opposition but of resistance and held that fanzine publishing was a form of implied social criticism.

We can let Rastelli himself give us a history lesson on fanzines in Quebec since 1968 and a background to the field, as he saw it, before his creation of *Fish Piss*. His article for the Expozine catalogue in 2012 (also in French, of course) is a great overview:

> What marks the underground press publications of the sixties as a precursor to what's come since is in how they were edited, published and read by and for young people with few restrictions on format and content... A good example of this new genre was *Logos*, published in Montreal in the late sixties. Even though *Logos* was primarily English, it supported the separatist Front de Liberation du Quebec (FLQ)... With underground comics, psychedelic art, articles on rock music and ads for local record stores, cafés, and bookstores, *Logos* used a formula still recognizable in many zines around the world.

The alternative campus newspapers of the 1960s graduated a whole generation of radicalized and sensitive publishing styles to the wider media in the 1970s. Rastelli sites *National Lampoon, The Village Voice,* and *Rolling Stone,* which started more like zines before becoming mainstream, as prominent examples. Also in the 1970s was the rise of punk and an influential DIY (anti)cultural movement. Among those zines published in Montreal were *Surfin Bird, Red She Said, Drug Lovers,* and Rick Trembles' *Sugar Diet.* Some of the notable US zines coming out of this era were *Search & Destroy* (later *Re / Search*), *Maximum RocknRoll, Raw!,* and *Flipside.*

As a response to the perception that *Maximum RocknRoll* was becoming too elitist, the Chicago-based publication *Punk Planet* formed as a newsprint zine in 1994 and "treated punk rock as an idea, not a sound." Kyle Ryan on the AV Club blog states why *Punk Planet's* demise, in 2007 after eighty issues, matters:

> Using punk's antagonist spirit as a guiding principle, *Punk Planet* transcended stereotypes to chronicle the progressive underground community, from thoughtful band interviews to exceptionally thorough investigative features. Over the course of thirteen years, *Punk Planet* became heavily in-fluential beyond the increasingly small world of independent publishing, but eventually many com-plained about its high price, perfect binding, and a perceived over-attention to layout and style (such as the inclusion of page numbers and a table of contents), which had to

a certain extent moved it away from the traditional punk aesthetic.

In the same way *Punk Planet* evolved Rastelli emphasizes that the punk zines coming out of Montreal were part of the transition to more established alternative weeklies that rose in the 1990s:

> Zines up until that era were predominantly collective projects, with several writers and artists pooling time and resources to print zines that in form were not much different from 'real' magazines. Some notable Quebec zines of this type were the long-running *Mainmise*, and *Rectangle*. These writers and artists helped create the first wave of alternative free weeklies that were published between 1985 and 1990 (ie. *Voir*) which were found [until recently] in most cities in North America.

Lauren Alexandria Brown riffs off Virginia Woolf's book title in her article "A Zine of One's Own: DIY and Alternative Expression among the Beats and the Riot Grrrls" in which she examines the Riot Grrrl movement of Generation X and how zines were such an important mode of expression and community-building at a time when mainstream culture was embracing MTV and *Seventeen* magazine. The Riot Grrrl movement was founded after the commercialization of punk exposed its inherent patriarchal structure.

> The Riot Grrrl movement of the eighties and nineties subverted the punk movement and combated anti-feminism, using their words, music and cut-and-paste skills to assert both their collective feminism and their individual identities.... The Riot Grrrl Manifesto speaks to the desire of an accessible process and medium through which to distribute these ideas—primarily through the creation of zines and girl bands.

Some of these zines were *Queer Fish, Reject Gene, Ballroom Etiquette, kittybrat, secret language, soiled princess, Glamour Queen, Racecar, Rome Wasn't Built in a Day, Baby Fat, Pressure Points, Lucid Nation, You Can't Bring Me Down* and *Oh Boy*. As Brown writes, "Girl zines were and are still important because they tackle issues that seem more important to girls such as body image, sexuality and violence, as well as pushing the boundaries of genre and gender." These zines were a public forum to discuss private topics.

The most significant and influential zine in North America in the 1980s was *Factsheet Five*, founded in 1982 by Mike Gunderloy, as a two-page publication. It grew to become a comprehensive guide to zines and alternative publications. *Factsheet Five* featured an abundance of zines—complete with price, capsule reviews, and ordering information. It was more about cataloguing than critical reviews of publications; it was a place for interested creators to write to each other, trade, and form a community centered around zines. Many young zine makers found their tribe when they sent a few bucks and stamps to other zine makers across the continent after reading their review in *Factsheet Five*. Gunderloy's involvement ended with issue #44, published in 1991. R. Seth Friedman took over, publishing the zine for five years in San Francisco, until issue #64 in 1998. Duncombe gives a history of the tension between the first and second iterations of the zine. The original *Factsheet Five*, under the editorship of Gunderloy was a zine, and "reading it you definitely got the sense that you were *inside* of something." The next generation was not a zine—it was a magazine about zines which was "packaged to be sold in the chain stores of your local shopping mall." Basically, it became a capitalist venture. "Mike's zine broke down the insular subworlds of independent publishing in an effort to combine them into a larger underground community, Seth's magazine sold the underground to the masses.... Instead of access into cultural *production*, what Seth was promoting was access into cultural *consumption*." However, Friedman got national distribution and media attention for zines, and today the New York State Library holds The Factsheet Five Collection.

A well-documented example of the legacy of *Factsheet Five* is the correspondence between comic artists Julie Doucet (*Dirty Plotte*) in Montreal and John Porcellino (*King-Cat*) in the US who met through the pages of *Factsheet Five*. Porcellino writes that the magazine "reviewed zines—odd, self-published little booklets made by freaks and weirdos and housewives and grandpas. There were cooking zines, poetry zines, political zines, music zines… you name it. And comics. A lot of comics." He describes meeting Doucet through their pages after seeing a review of *Dirty Plotte* listed: "If you sent your zine in for review, they'd send you a copy of the FF with your review in it in return. Then if you were me, you'd sit with each new issue and pore over it for days, bracketing cool-sounding mags, making little notes in the margins." This mailing zines back and forth established a network of independent artists.

The 1990s was considered a revolution in zine making. This was due to a perfect storm of photocopy technology being widely available at easily accessible locations like Kinkos (or Copie 2000 in my case), which allowed for small print runs and hands-on control, cheap design software, as well as a distribution system which piggybacked on alternative music—including that of *Fish Piss*, which was eventually distributed by the Tower Records chain. In the 1990s, just as grunge became alternative music, so too did zines become part of the zeitgeist; they were *part* of alternative culture. As Rastelli says, "Even when a zine featured the works of several writers and artists, it became increasingly common for one person to take on nearly all aspects of publishing, editing, layout, production, and distribution. Some well-known American zines were *Answer Me!, Thrift Score, Duplex Planet, Temp Slave, Cometbus, Fucktooth*, and *Beer Frame*."

Montreal was uniquely situated within the field for the zine revolution. Rastelli explains:

> One characteristic that set Quebec zines apart in that era was the influence felt not just from the American zine scene but from European zines. Silkscreened covers and printing appeared in Quebec zines quite a bit earlier than elsewhere in North America, and the alternative comics and graphics scenes adopted some of the harder styles and visual aesthetics of European publishers such as Le Dernier Cri.

In Montreal, there were many comics with silk-screened covers, mostly printed by Simon Bossé's company Mille Putois (which began as a collaborative comic zine with Alexandre Lafleur), but also by Leyla Majeri and Seripop. The study of francophone mini comics at this time could be the subject of another book altogether. However, there were other zines with silkscreen covers and political and literary content. *Food Not Lawns* (2001) was run out of a working group of QPIRG McGill and Concordia (Quebec Public Interest Research Group) "because lawns symbolize much of what is perverse and contradictory about modern North American capitalist society." Designer Kevin Yuen Kit Lo teamed up with John W. Stuart to produce the perfect-bound graphic design zine *Four Minutes to Midnight.* Issues 1 through 5 were created as part of Lo's MA thesis at the London College of Printing in 2004. They produced an all Expozine edition in 2011.

Jeff Chapman, aka Ninjalicious, ran one of the most important zines of the nineties out of Pickering, Ontario.

It was called *Infiltration: the zine about going places you're not supposed to go* (1996-2005). The history of this zine corresponds almost exactly with *Fish Piss* and is an obvious influence. It was devoted to the art of urban exploration, a sort of interior tourism that allowed the curious-minded to discover behind-the-scenes sights and have a lot of free fun. On reviewing *Infiltration*, Rastelli wrote, "I always thought of it as the perfect example of a zine: it focused on a subject that no one else wrote about, and did it in a way that made for excellent reading whether you were an explorer yourself or not." *Infiltration* featured editorials, exploring advice and information, articles on recent expeditions, and interviews, all illustrated with maps, pictures, and diagrams. The zine has been called "life-changing" and did much to herald in the urban exploration movement. The final issue of *Infiltration* (#25) came out in June, 2005. That same year saw the publication of *Access All Areas: A User's Guide to the Art of Urban Exploration*. Chapman passed away the same year at the age of thirty-one.

Broken Pencil was founded the year before *Fish Piss* by Hal Niedzviecki and began as Canada's answer to *Factsheet Five*. Its tagline changed over the first dozen issues as it tried to figure out its role in the North American field of alternative publications. It started as "The Guide to Alternative Culture in Canada" but the title changed, perhaps because of the letter Rastelli writes in issue #6 complaining about the declaration of primacy and completeness in that "The" when it did not even cover French zines, or much of anything in Quebec. In the review of *Broken Pencil* in issue #63 of *Factsheet Five* (1998), this haggling over one word was mentioned: "BP grapples with many of the same complaints leveled against F5. Is it '*The* Guide to Alternative Culture in Canada' or just *a* guide. Or does it matter? Of course not. It's in the doing, not the wording. And BP both does enough and has words enough to encourage community in an often-fragmented Canadian scene." By issue #14 the tagline read "Zine Culture in Canada and the World" which was definitely more inclusive but ambiguous. Finally, the editors settled on "The Magazine of Zine Culture and the Independent Arts." So, it was not a zine about zines, it was a *magazine* about independent art and culture. This may have been because the editors focused less on zines and more on articles about culture, books, movies, but certainly always based in a DIY spirit. They defined "zine" in their masthead: "What makes a zine a zine is its dedication to the independent transference of thought on a non-commercial basis." Publications were listed by region at first, so everything coming out of Montreal was grouped together. Early on the editors called on me to provide more Montreal content so I started writing reviews of chapbooks and mini comics which helped me get to know the local scene better. The other contributor they asked from Montreal was Louis Rastelli. We also both wrote reviews in *Fish Piss*. So, there was cross-pollination for sure. And *Broken Pencil* reviewed *Fish Piss* many times.

Another contemporary Canadian zine was *Kiss Machine* (Toronto) founded by Emily Pohl-Weary and Paola Poletto, which lasted eighteen issues (2000-2008). In an effort to highlight the surrealism inherent in day-to-day life, each "literary conga line" featured two seemingly discordant themes, which were determined in-part by their contributors. The *Toronto Star* dubbed it "a community on paper" and "one of four indie magazines to watch out for." Pohl-Weary has said a lack of female representation was one of the reasons she started the zine: "When you're making your own zine, you get to control everything. You get to decide the message." Kiss Machine Presents was an imprint offshoot of the zine which published the first comic version of *Skim*, which would become the award-winning and breakthrough graphic novel from cousins Mariko Tamaki and Jillian Tamaki.

In the 2000s, the internet, though still not the juggernaut of today, began to dominate, and many zinesters turned to ezines, or fansites, or MySpace pages. They found each other on Live Journal accounts instead of in the pages of *Factsheet Five*. Perhaps the internet sounded the death knell for zines. However, the way Rastelli saw it in 2010 he was "baffled at any notion that people should stop making zines. Expressing yourself on your own, when no other media around you is reflecting your reality, will always be pertinent. This isn't being replaced by Facebook or Twitter or blogs, because those are very fleeting, ephemeral expressions, and rarely involves the care one takes in deciding what to write down for posterity in a zine." The fact that zines are printed and folded and stapled means there is an investment of labour in making a zine, as opposed to typing directly into the ether, which means different decisions are made as to content. Zines are not simply portals for information, they are art objects in themselves, they are cultural artifacts made carefully by human hands and will "convey today's styles and sensibilities to the future long after the hosting plans for today's websites have expired." Rastelli makes the claim that zines aren't dead—they've just become art.

The effect on readers of this tactile medium is provided by the students in Allison Piepmeier's class. In her article "Why Zines Matter: Materiality and the Creation of Embodied Community," she points to the success of zines as a product of their materiality.

> Every time I teach a class about zines, a significant percentage of the students begin making their own. Many of them have never heard of zines, but when I bring in a pile for them to flip through and take home, they become inspired. This doesn't happen if I require them to read a published anthology of zines such as *A Girl's Guide to Taking Over the World*; getting their hands on actual zines is necessary to ignite this creative urge. My students have been inspired to become part of the zine community because

of physical encounters with actual zines, not by reading anthologized zines.

But what about the temporality of physical zines? They are not the same as a daily newspaper whose news is outdated the morning after, or the blog that is unreadable when the link expires. One method of collecting these zines for posterity is to give them a spine and an ISBN (International Standard Book Number) and allow them space on the bookstore shelf. This is what I began to do with Conundrum Press. I discovered zines by Canadian artists reviewed in *Broken Pencil*—such as those by Emily Holton, Ian Sullivan Cant, Elisabeth Belliveau or cover star Shary Boyle—collected them into books, and called them "graphic novels," which was a new category for libraries and bookstores and was still a very loose and amorphous term at the time. This was a very conscious mandate and one that morphed with the development of the definition of the graphic novel field. I had some interesting discussions with readers I met at the New York Art Book Fair in 2009. I met a rare book dealer who encouraged me to hold onto my zines because they would be worth a lot of money someday as rare books. But I also had a librarian tell me to sell my zine collection now because they were the hot *objects du jour* and libraries were just starting their zine collections.

Fish Piss did not play by the traditional rules of publishing fields, as outlined in John B. Thompson's *Books in the Digital Age* and based on Bourdieu's fields of cultural production. Thompson outlines four sources for capital available to a publisher: economic capital (access to funds), human capital (access to staff), intellectual capital (access to rights), and symbolic capital (the status or brand recognition of a publishing house). Success in small press publishing and zines cannot be measured in economic terms. Thompson places the small press within the social structure of publishing fields. Larger publishers deal in economic and human capital whereas smaller presses and zines privilege the intangible asset of symbolic capital. "Symbolic capital is best understood as the accumulated prestige, recognition and respect accorded to certain individuals or institutions.... For publishers are not just employers and financial risk-takers: they are also cultural mediators... their imprint is a 'brand,' a marker of distinction in a highly competitive field." Although *Fish Piss* in its later issues would trade on its symbolic capital, it operated totally outside this paradigm. The idea of a publishing "industry" was totally anathema to its values. In fact, it could be argued the DIY aesthetic forms its own publishing field: valuing community engagement over distribution, valuing openness and diversity over sales figures.

But did it sell? Well, before a Tower Records distribution deal, *Fish Piss* was building its symbolic capital but also making sales. In a 1998 interview, Rastelli talks about "selling out" by leaving copies of issue #3 at the chain bookstore Chapters: "It was insane! They sold forty-seven of them there alone, just in that one store. I asked them, 'Is that more or less normal for a magazine?' They said, 'No way! No other magazine has ever sold that much at Chapters.' I said, 'Now come on, *Time*, I'm sure you sell more *Time* magazines.' They said, 'Oh no, maybe ten.' That's a lot of people looking at all that stuff and picking something local. Which is great. That's partly why I put *Fish Piss* together."

On Rastelli, in the anniversary issue (#50) of *Broken Pencil*, the editors wrote: "*Fish Piss* was Canada's most important zine of the late 1990s. It not only gave voice to the country's most interesting indie scene, it also gave a home to emerging, unforgettable talent." It is safe to say the *Fish Piss* brand had enormous symbolic capital.

Why Montreal?

An examination of any publishing enterprise in Montreal must add a fifth type of capital, linguistic capital, which is an addition Lina Shoumarova makes in her 2007 MA thesis on linguistic properties of the book-publishing field in Montreal. She interviewed French and English publishers (Conundrum Press included), and examined their contact points. To describe the unique cultural space of Montreal, where these publishers interact, Shoumarova uses the term "contact zone," which was coined by Mary Louise Pratt: "Contact zones emerged from the complexities of the cultural, political, and economic configurations set in place by colonialism and represent spaces of contestation, rather than harmonious communication. Despite the tension, or probably precisely because of it, the contact zones are also characterized by a highly creative potential that gives rise to hybrid forms of perception and culture-making."

Traditionally, a linguistic publishing field would operate within a rubric of geographic limitation (books published in English would be sold in English-speaking countries), the selling of foreign rights (translations), or through partnerships with foreign publishers. Again, *Fish Piss* operates outside this field. Unlike a magazine that translates its own text and formats them side by side on the page (such as *En Route*) *Fish Piss* is truly bilingual; its comics and essays, poems, and stories exist on the page in the language they were written, without translation. It is assumed the (local) audience is as bilingual as the editor. This is the contact zone to which Shoumarova refers: the two solitudes meeting on the page, or at least an audience willing to embrace "linguistic otherness." For Shoumarova, language shapes a cultural field. Montreal is an "intellectual nodal point" and *Fish Piss* becomes an "inter-cultural dialogue."

Rastelli hints at this linguistic capital when he states that he was drawn into the scene, after working on *RearGarde* and *Flaming Poutine*, "by what was unmistakably a Montreal way of writing. And what is an unmistakably Montreal way of writing? Nothing more than the little quirks in the grammar that are peculiar to this city. Stuff you'd notice in an instant when you read it, since you could read it in your head just as easily as you'd talk it. In these zines we got to read our own accent for pretty much the first time."

Montreal has historically been placed as the other. Being within Quebec, it is outside the North American English hegemony, but being a cosmopolitan city, it is outside the French hegemony of rural Quebec. Before the Quiet Revolution of the 1960s, Montreal was part of an isolated province, run predominantly by the Catholic Church. In the forties and fifties, leading up to the expansion, Montreal was known as The City of Sin, where gambling and the allure of Lili St. Cyr and strip clubs were prevalent and ignored by the corrupt municipal leaders. As William Weintraub describes in his book *City Unique*, it was also the home of Oscar Peterson and a thriving jazz scene, where writers Mordecai Richler and Mavis Gallant were at the beginning of their illustrious careers. The anglophones were the bosses, the francophones the workers. It was a skewed power dynamic. But since the 1970s there has been a paradigm shift, with francophones moving to the suburbs and anglophones starting to occupy the vacant spaces of the downtown core. Then came two referendums in 1980 and 1995 which crippled the economy because many anglophones took their businesses to more hospitable climes. The almost-too-close-to-call referendum of 1995 was the nail in the coffin for any hope of reviving an infrastructure for anglophone culture in Quebec. The *No* side, which voted not to separate Quebec from the rest of Canada, won over the *Yes*, which voted to make Quebec an independent state, by 50.58% to 49.42%. This meant Montreal was primed to become a city unique once again; anyone who chose to stay was committed to a lifestyle of foraging in urban decay to make art happen—in other words, a lifestyle of bohemia. But they were also committed to a new economic paradigm, outside the traditional trappings of the state (except for the replacement of arts grants with welfare), one which the specificity of the contact zones of Montreal made possible.

In his essay "Tracing Out an Anglo-Bohemia" Geoff Stahl writes on the music scene: "As part of a social and aesthetic lineage which extends from salons in nineteenth-century Paris to the happenings in 1960s New York, Montreal musical life is solidly entrenched within a matrix of mobile and durable social, spatial and cultural practices which have always determined the means through which bohemians make a habitable world out of seemingly inhospitable urban decay, economic decline and cultural detritus." Efrim Manuel Menuck, *Fish Piss* contributor and co-founder of the hugely influential band Godspeed You! Black Emperor is interviewed by Stahl and has this to say on the topic: "Montreal's a place that's always losing its charm. It's a corrupt city in a corrupt province, where somehow the light rings loudly anyhow... We're very vocal about the fact that we're from Montreal. That's part of our schtick. It's conscious on that level. It's about being really into this city and into the circumstances that have allowed us to exist."

Of course, the economic recession that followed also hurt the francophone artists working under the radar. As Rastelli states: "The reality in Quebec is that most of the francophone artists wanted to take the opportunity of being in a magazine with wide North American distribution to publish in English. Clearly most of the readership was English. Whether text or comics, *Fish Piss* was never more than one quarter French, if that. I personally liked to have some French, even if minimal, in there, just to let the world know that Montreal is a bilingual city."

Spoken-word artist, and my roommate for a time, Catherine Kidd articulated the environment of Montreal in her 1997 interview for *Impure: Reinventing the Word*: "I think of Montreal as a primordial ooze. It seems like a lot of people come here to steep in their own creative juices." In fact, there is a whole chapter in which the editors Vince Tinguely and Victoria Stanton interview both francophone and anglophone writers and performers on what makes the city unique for hybrid forms of art. The title of the book comes from a comment made by Nathalie Derome referring to the "potluck" that is the Montreal cultural community. "Impure" implies a hybrid, whether in performance style, mixed genres, part poetry, part stand up, part theatre of the absurd, or even the idea of a more open-minded audience. But "impure" also refers to, or is created from, the co-mixing of languages. Other interviewees have more to say about the city:

> Leah Vineberg: "You know if you listen closely enough, when you're speaking onstage in the most codified manner, in a weird way you're speaking to your fellow codified friends."

> Jeremiah Wall: "English is a renegade language in Quebec. English society has to make itself wherever it can, set up the tents and do the circus, it's like the circus is in town... One of the things that characterizes Montreal's scene is that you

don't have a large commercial publication presence here. [People] are not meeting and saying, 'I just published with the big publishing company.' They're saying, 'Oh I went to this stage and I did that and we were in this magazine and we started this series... This is the bohemian sink."

Corey Frost: "I think that the scene in Montreal wouldn't exist if there weren't so many unemployed people, or people who were willing to live on next to nothing and involve themselves voluntarily, and just have that sensibility of being slightly counterculture because you're not participating in the production of capital."

Alex Boutros: "In Montreal there has been a lot of crossover. You'd get someone like Tawhida Tanya Evanson playing Yawp! and playing Unusual Suspects and doing Girlspit, and she could move. And I think that freedom to move from venue to venue is very unique to Montreal.

Heather O'Neill: "New stuff always works well in Montreal, as far as the avant-garde goes... The name Montreal has a significance, especially in the States. What does manage to get out is of such high quality and so original. Because there are so few presses and it's such a challenge, the people who stick with it usually have strong talent."

Of course, I need to clarify that for the purposes of this book I am mostly referring to the neighbourhoods of the Plateau and Mile End in Montreal, which are where most of the venues and participants lived. Boulevard St-Laurent runs North/South and splits the city into a predominantly West anglophone side and predominantly East francophone side. The Plateau / Mile End straddles this street; it is a liminal zone, with many artists on both sides. Mile End was the traditional Jewish Quarter (the Saint Urbain Street of Mordecai Richler) before it was Greek, then Orthodox Hasidic with a mix of immigrants and languages in the 1990s. In fact, Rastelli lived on Clark for the years he spent creating *Fish Piss*, one block west of St-Laurent. In his novel he writes, "Here in the Plateau it's sort of like a small town in the middle of a big city." Or consider his description of the density of artists in the neighbourhood: "It's sort of as if the Plateau is our house, and of course you're bound to run into your relatives on the way to the bathroom."

Montreal is also well situated as a contact zone for comics, or as they are commonly called in Quebec, *bandes dessinées*. Due to the confluence of American underground influences from the counterculture of the 1960s (R. Crumb) through to the avant-garde of *RAW!* in the 1980s (Spiegelman), the mainstream Franco-Belgian tradition (*Tintin*), and the alternative graphzines of Europe (Le Dernier Cri), Montreal comic artists are unique in the field. One nodal point created in the 1990s between French and English comic artists was the public event called the Comic Jam, or *bd en direct*. The first *Fish Piss* cover artist Mavreas recalls:

> Rupert Bottenberg started putting these things together. The first one was at some dingy little bar, and we all sat at tables and drew and passed the things to each other. It was interesting because these jams basically put a whole bunch of us misfits together in the same place. Communities formed and friendships were made. There was never one word exchanged about what someone *should* do with their work. The boundaries were very fluid.

These jams were public events which added another level of interaction since "rock and roll was served later on."

The story of artist Jack Dylan exemplifies the lifecycle of the bohemian paradigm perfectly, though it came at the tail end of the *Fish Piss* generation. Coming from Stratford, Ontario, twenty-year-old Andrew Attard changed his name and moved to Montreal in 2003 for the lifestyle:

> None of us had jobs, but everything had come together. I thought, *wow I'm living the dream with my art friends in a warehouse in a cool city, and I can just make art all day*. But it was within a few months of this that I realized how terrible it was. *I'm a poor person now, and this place is really messy,*

> *and it's going to take me at least ten years to crawl out of this. No one's cleaning. This place is a dump.*
>
> It was a rude awakening.

In an article for GODBERD in 2018, an uncredited high school friend provides an exposé of Dylan:

> Jack gave his best friend from Stratford, Graham Van Pelt (of the bands Miracle Fortress and Think About Life) the hard sell to come join him, to be a musician in Montreal. It wasn't too hard of a decision for Graham because he, like many other young musicians at the time, revered Montreal's Constellation Records and Alien8 Recordings....

They found a cheap loft at 6674 Esplanade, in an industrial dead-end zone of Mile End. Van Pelt describes the living arrangements in an issue of Dylan's *Park Towers* zine:

> We crafted bedrooms for ourselves, with varying degrees of success. Some ended up with cozy roofed nooks, others with shanty-town skid-wood walls draped with cookware and the odd cleaning implement.... I didn't exactly make my room a home until some rather scrupulous friend came in to say, 'Well this is a bit of a hole.'...We didn't quite get around to installing proper bathing facilities for, say, five months. Instead, each of us

developed our own personal relationship with the local YMCA and its regulars.

A more bohemian living arrangement, I cannot imagine. The tenants needed to make a living, so they turned their living space into a venue, in the tradition of bohemian communities. The previous tenants had left up several adjustable signs donning their business name. "We were free to rearrange the sign letters in any way we saw fit. After several permutations which included *Électrique Actors Repent* and *Eat Nader,* we settled on *Electric Tractor,* a name which we were at a loss to outdo. [The venue] began to play host to local and touring musical acts, with a few hippie-poetry-weed-dolphin-love nights thrown in at random.... Of course, the sustainability of it all was questionable."

Dylan explains that they hosted some early literature readings. "We had one poetry reading, and I started reading a poem that I had been doing to great acclaim in Stratford and London, but as soon as I was reading in Montreal I realized, *Oh this is a much more sophisticated crowd.* I could feel it just *bombing*... I realized people in big cities have real addictions, playing at this Kerouacian character...in the real world it was pathetic to play at it." This wake-up call didn't deter him from continuing a literary magazine named after a fictional publishing imprint for his pulp fiction cover paintings. *Park Towers* (2004) was in format, content, and design (with silkscreen covers) obviously influenced by *Fish Piss.* The three main conditions for a bohemian community to exist were all present here: middle-class WASPs slumming it, a small DIY publication, and a cheap venue.

Dylan realized it would be more interesting to host musicians, and he would fill the space with bands like AIDS Wolf, Chinese Stars, Les Georges Leningrad, "which was a total sound, noise and liquor violation. We were such an obvious target for the police, but we somehow got away with it." After finding a new venue in Griffintown and naming it *Friendship Cove,* Dylan learned from his experiences and started making posters to advertise it. His reputation improved by doing the posters for POP Montreal. Then he moved to Toronto to become artistic director for the Toronto magazine *Corporate Knights.* Before moving to New York permanently, he emptied most of his old portfolios, illustrations, and paintings into a dumpster and walked away from bohemia. He entered the fast-paced magazine world, had a cover in *The New Yorker*, and dinner with the Obamas. For all intents and purposes Andrew Attard had made it. But when asked to look back at his Montreal days compared to his Toronto and New York days, he said it felt like the Montreal days were someone else's life. Montreal was "unrealistic," while going to school in Toronto and holding multiple jobs in New York was "like a normal person." Did his Montreal years matter to him? He fools himself into thinking they don't, but at the same time he gives himself away in hindsight: "I realize now it was really in the strength of my stupid posters that my whole world opened up… God! everything good in my life has come from selling posters!"

Ian McGillis, in his retrospective essay in the 2017 anniversary issue of *The Montreal Review of Books*, writes: "One doesn't wish to romanticize poverty, but the thing is, when it allows you to do what you want to do, it doesn't feel like poverty. In Y2K-era Montreal you could live the writing life with the feeling that you had entered a kind of culture-friendly Narnia. You were free to experiment, make mistakes, work at your own pace…"

A review of Rastelli's novel is in keeping with the idea that he was a part of things but also was an objective observer, he could never be just a tourist in bohemia because he had a day job: "Every good bohemia needs its chroniclers, people who are of the scene but in crucial ways a little outside it too. People who, among the chaos and the excess and the occasional lassitude and the living for the moment, keep enough perspective to get it all down." Rastelli describes the milieu of his novel and the bohemian atmosphere of the times but also credits how his day job fueled the zine:

> Low rent, easy welfare, high unemployment, pre-internet, four universities parked around the mountain, there may have been a higher-than-average quantity of writers and artists and musicians than other places. I was one of the only people I knew working a day job at an office. I didn't sleep much, keeping up with all my friends who mostly hung

> out at Miami and other bars every single night. But as per the nineties zinester cliché, I got to use the office photocopiers and fax machines and mailroom. I had a great boss who was a patron of the arts, so he'd actually encourage me to do my projects as long as I always got the actual job done.

In the late 1990s and early 2000s, Montreal anglophones invested their time and energy creating their own culture under the radar because they were essentially invisible: to other Montrealers, the rest of Canada, and to the world. They were able to "stew in their creative juices" until it all blew up and the mainstream media came calling, when Montreal became the "New Seattle." As Ryan Bigge explains in his article for *Broken Pencil*, "Searching for Breakfast in Bohemia":

> They described and reinforced notions surrounding their creative community through a shared language about culture and art. The instrumental post-rock hymns of Godspeed provide a soundtrack of urban decay while writings like [Jonathan Goldstein's] *Lenny Bruce is Dead* or the zine *Fish Piss* articulate the habits and attitudes of Montreal's English outcasts... It's easy to over-romanticize Montreal, but its bohemian cityspace offers a location to project our cultural desires, an asset too valuable to calculate.

Why 1990s?

Fish Piss was a product of a very specific time and place. Last chapter dealt with what made the contact zone of Montreal so unique. But what was so special about those times? For Montreal, the number-one determining factor for culture, especially English at that time, was the 1995 Quebec Referendum. That was the Big Bang for so many artistic endeavors including *Fish Piss* and Conundrum. In a 2016 article Montreal culture critic Lucinda Catchlove writes: "The referendum in '95 saw Quebec vote to remain in Canada (barely) and, with the new millennium creeping closely with apocalyptic portent, the past and future circled each other uncertainly. Nonetheless, many Montreal artists found inspiration in the dread. In the neighborhood of Mile End, with its mix of abandoned industrial spaces, rich cultural influences, and blend of the orthodox and innovative, a new wave of artists began to add to the area's already fecund mythology." Norsola Johnson, who played cello with Molasses, Godspeed You! Black Emperor, and Ratchet Orchestra, states, "It was a very melancholy time. Instead of angst, a rage and desire to change things, we became more reflective about the decline of society as a whole... We never even questioned it. You want to make something happen, you have to do it yourself." And it was the music scene that really took advantage of the economy. Writers and comic artists can use pens and paper, but musicians need to gather, they need to perform and practice, they need loft spaces to function, and the vacancy rate in this former textile district allowed for it to happen.

That same year, printmaker and chef Kiva Stimac and her partner, Godspeed bassist Mauro Pezzente, moved into one of these spaces on Van Horne. "When you have the space, people will come," says Stimac, who moved to Montreal as a student. "My family is from Detroit. Detroit is a great example of [how] when you have nothing, you still build something from the ashes." These ideals would help create venues, cultural nodes needed to fuel bohemia, thereby turning Mile End into "one of the most internationally heralded, culturally vibrant neighborhoods in the world."

Another unique circumstance, specific to Montreal, was the unprecedented Ice Storm in January, 1998. Power lines broke and over a thousand transmission towers collapsed in chain reactions under the weight of the ice, leaving more than four million people without electricity, and therefore no heat. The city came to a standstill as the temperature plummeted. Or as Rastelli described it, "very slowly and beautifully, ice accumulated over the city." His news headline in #4 stated: "City enjoys 'week of the century' as army, police and ordinary people ensure that not a single person is cold, hungry, or homeless." The event occurred between issues #3 and #4 of *Fish Piss* and Rastelli devoted his editorial in #4 to the natural phenomenon that crippled the city and made everyone more conscious of the structural network that pieces a city together and the human network of friends and neighbours that lie underneath:

> No one had expected that this icy weather would slowly, bit by bit, cripple all the machines. And, until it happened, no one realized how many machines we usually depend on. Then, no one realized how easily we could do without them... It could've been far simpler had life in this city kept on as it was during the big shutdown, when electricity was out indefinitely and people did what came naturally. It turned out that what we do naturally is pretty damn good—we help each other, we entertain each other, and as all the old magazines got read three times over, the people in the shelters or at friends' houses were quite ready for something new to read. Especially something which they could relate to, something which reflected this warm, well-fed bullshit-free life everyone was suddenly living. Especially when the rest of the media was busy sensationalizing it all as some 'crisis' for the sake of a dramatic story to sell.

The third defining event that shaped the *Fish Piss* generation was the Quebec City Summit of the Americas, from April 20–22, 2001. Issue #7 (2002) devotes a fifty-page special feature to the personal stories of the Quebec Summit, based on interviews Rastelli did with a dozen people who were there plus an official civil-liberties observer, as well as his extensive research of local newspapers, zines, television coverage, and "guerrilla" video. Rastelli states that in his opinion, "No one [he] spoke to broke the law in any way." Before that weekend, I remember groups of friends planning to get together and hire busses to protest in Quebec City, three hours away. From the news, we knew they had been building a three-metre-high concrete and wire fence around a large section of La Colline Parlementaire that encircled the meeting site. From the beginning, the authorities indicated their intent to use very intensive security measures to restrict the ability of protesters to approach the area where the summit was to take place, in light of a well-known previous incident in Seattle. The Quebec City protests (called A20) were one of the largest anti-globalization demonstrations to that point. The authorities tear-gassed the protestors. The incident disillusioned and politicized many Montreal artists, and those politics seeped into their art.

Of course, on a more global scale during this time-period was *fin de siècle* ennui and anxiety surrounding the Y2K bug. There was a real fear in the mainstream press that all the computers around the world would shut down as

1999 changed to 2000 because their date clocks were not programmed correctly. It seemed ludicrous to me at the time, but the fear was heightened by so many other world events: Clinton had been impeached but remained in office; Lucien Bouchard, leader of the separatist Parti Québécois, was still leading Quebec; the Columbine High School massacre set a horrifying precedent in the US; the human population of the world surpassed six billion; and there was even a total eclipse of the sun. There was a real sense that all this had to come to an end, that we couldn't go on living like this forever.

Chuck Klosterman in his book *The Nineties* really captures what it was like to live as a Gen X person, in a liminal zone between a pre-internet and post-internet world. He calls the Boomers and the Gen Xers "interlocked generations" because they are the only people in history to witness the shift in real time, to be the only "fluent translators of Before and After." The internet, which came on gradually, then suddenly in the 1990s, "exponentially expanded the parameters of external existence while decreasing the material size of interior existence. It allowed any person to simultaneously possess two competing identities—one actual and one virtual." *Fish Piss* also straddles this time of Before and After, but its physical construct as a zine made it almost a time capsule for a generation's angst.

The history of printing technology tightly parallels the communication techniques of alternative culture. The 1990s witnessed a "revolution" in zine making due to the advancement of photocopying. But what led to this moment? By establishing the printing press in 1439, Guttenberg was the first European to use movable type and made the Bible available for anyone to interpret. This was democracy in action but was met with resistance from the rulers, those with control of the "media," in this case the scripture. Visionary William Blake famously refined the process of relief etching (or illuminated printing) in 1794 to produce his illuminated poetry books *Songs of Innocence* and *Songs of Experience*, creating the first self-published art books. In Alessandro Ludovico's *Post-Digital Print: The Mutation of Publishing since 1894*, we find a chapter on the history of alternative publishing reflecting the evolution of print. It starts with a quote from André Breton, one of the founders of the 1920s Surrealist movement, "One publishes to find comrades!" Ludovico states, "This short statement brilliantly embodies the spirit of early avant-garde publishing, as well as that of independent publishing later in the twentieth century." Of course, it also embodies the spirit of *Fish Piss*.

The use of print in the twentieth century avant-garde begins with the Italian Futurists whose bold statements were distributed through magazines such as *Poesia* (1905), the international journal of the Futurist movement. *Lacerba* magazine (1914) "featured a rethinking of typographical composition... pushing to the very limit the possibilities of black-and-white letterpress printing." Parallel to this was the Dada movement which produced a number of journals including Tristan Tzara's *Dada* (1917) printed on letterpress.

These publications can be seen as "the ancestors of the later zines." The Dadaists attempted to exploit the experimental possibilities of the printing machine, even using collages and photomontages. The next big leap in technology, with the advent of electricity, was the mimeograph or "mimeo," which allowed for underground publishing. The trade unionists of the Industrial Workers of the World embraced the mimeograph in the 1930s, finding in it the "ideal medium for fostering freedom of expression and ideas." Because it was lightweight and compact, it could be moved and avoid confiscation and censorship. Post-war, the mimeo was co-opted by offices, schools, and church bulletins, as well as being used to print *Beatitude*, the first Beat zine. It made cheap, quick copies, at a reasonable quality. In the 1950s, the mimeo began to be used by science fiction aficionados to make fanzines. A community around the alternative press was born. Fluxist Ken Friedman was the founding editor of *New York Correspondence School Weekly Breeder*, a zine from the 1960s which circulated artist address lists and was instrumental in the birth of mail art and led to the Canadian art collective General Idea's publication of *FILE Megazine* which went global. At the same time in the Soviet Union the self-publishing Samizdat movement grew out of necessity, because of institutionalized disenfranchisement. Xerography, or what is commonly called "photocopying," was first marketed by Xerox in the 1960s for use in offices. The technology did not become available to the general public until the 1970s.

Specialty shops with photocopiers began to open and the punk movement embraced the technology to make cut-and-paste zines, but more importantly to re-appropriate the media and make it for themselves. In many ways, the production of the photocopied zine comes full circle to those first Bibles made by Guttenberg, allowing the public to make their own interpretations of the scripture.

The 1990s in Montreal saw the perfect circumstances for the rise of a printed zine like *Fish Piss*, a recession era that encompassed political upheaval, a referendum, and the Ice Storm, and culminated, or fizzled out, with Y2K. This was a time when creating your own media meant printing it, since digital was still in its infancy, the internet still had no advertising, and social media was a decade away. Louis Rastelli found himself in the right place at the right time and just took hold of the reins and held on.

What is a Bohemian?

Being a bohemian is to react against the values of the middle class, often the very class into which the actor has been born. The term originated in France at the height of the Romantic movement in the aftermath of defeat following the Napoleonic Wars from 1803-1815. There were a large number of well-educated aristocrats who had been stripped of their patronage and were left wandering the streets of Paris with very little to do. At the same time, the sons of shopkeepers and craftspeople found their skills irrelevant with the rise of industrialism. They flocked to the city and adopted a flamboyant lifestyle of living in garrets and frequenting cafés. The upstanding citizens of Paris were horrified at these layabouts and called them "bohemians," because the thought since Medieval times was that gypsies came from Bohemia (part of what is now the Czech Republic). Basically, in their minds, a gypsy was a transient character and not a positive influence.

Finding a definition for a bohemian is difficult because the term itself is so ambiguous. Researching this book, I could only find two works that even made the slightest attempt. The earliest and first book to tackle the subject was *Garrets and Pretenders: A History of Bohemianism in America* by Albert Parry (1933). As Parry points out, "Since bohemianism is pre-eminently a socio-literary phenomenon, the periods of its rise and decay coincided fairly well throughout the world, America included, with its cycles in France." Parry also addresses the idea that when bohemians rebel against the middle class, they make themselves classless: "bohemianism is not a class feature; its adherents are not a class because there is less of a hereditary character in their group than in any other group of society. Theirs is a temporary, flexible group. Very seldom are bohemians the sons and daughters of bohemians and begetters of bohemians in their turn… bohemians are declassed, as Marxians tell us." Parry also addresses the idea of authenticity, which is the opposite of the alienation that fuels the movement: "When madness, or its minor form, eccentricity, are pretended, bohemianism degenerates into flamboyancy, into a deliberate pose. Poe and Baudelaire were, perhaps, truer bohemians than Oscar Wilde and a Greenwich Villager." However, he admits it is often difficult to tell the difference: "bohemianism as such is too elusive, and the term has been too much abused, to enable a writer on the subject to draw rigid lines designating some men of art as sincere nomads and other men of art as pretenders." As Seigel writes in 1986, this figure came to have an important sociological role in society: "The phenomenon of the *artiste maudit* has served an important function for society as a whole, proving a kind of sacred and sacrificial figure who performs for others both the extravagant celebrations of life and the ritual subjection to destructive and irrational feelings that in primitive cultures were the subject of periodic rites of carnival, magic, and exorcism. All these considerations suggest that the avant-garde, like bohemianism, was seldom simply a rejection of the bourgeois world it declared to be its enemy."

But how does this translate to the bohemians of recent times? Well, they are still rebelling against their own class, and they are no more diverse than two hundred years ago. Like zine culture, bohemia is traditionally white, as Duncombe explains in *Notes from Underground*:

> White and raised in a relatively privileged position within the dominant culture, [zinesters] have since embarked on careers of deviance that have moved them to the edges of society; embracing downwardly mobile career aspirations, unpopular music and literary tastes, transgressive ideas about sexuality, unorthodox artistic sensibilities, and a politics resolutely outside the status quo... In short, zine writers and readers are what used to be called bohemians.

Perhaps the only real proper definition comes from the other seminal source on the subject, *On Bohemia: The Code of the Self-Exiled* (1990), edited by sociologists César Graña and Marigay Graña. Their clinical definition would be that bohemia is "a social mechanism for absorbing excess population until adequate status opportunities become available." Or put another way, "Bohemians are incubators of social change, protecting radical ideas from interference from the outside society until their time has come." However, they have also condensed all their research on the subject over its two hundred years to come up with an oft-repeated workable definition of a bohemia as filled with individuals who have an "attitude of dissent from the prevailing values of middle-class society—artistic, political, utilitarian, sexual—usually expressed in lifestyle and through a medium of the arts," and is centred around a café.

I would expand the idea of the café to the venue. This broadens the types of activities that can be considered bohemian. Bohemia needs its venues to exist. Also, I would clarify further to limit the scale and commitment of bohemia, to be a bohemian one needs to be invested in artistic pursuits in small groups, represented by a modest publication with a limited print run. These definitions apply to all the historically bohemian scenes outlined below and of course apply to the Montreal scene at the time of *Fish Piss.*

Of course, the word "scene" itself is problematic, as the Montreal academic Will Straw has pointed out: "The place of 'scene' within cultural analysis seems forever troubled by the variety of tasks it is called upon to perform. How useful is a term which designates both the effervescence of our favourite bar and the sum total of all global phenomena surrounding a subgenre of Heavy Metal music?" The term is a default label for an amorphous grouping of communities (such as those around *Fish Piss*) but can be either local or international (or sometimes both), and therefore not as specific as bohemia, which is centered around a venue and a small-scale publication.

In respect to venues creating scenes or scenes creating venues, Will Straw writes from Montreal just as the 1990s come to a close: "Are Laïka (previously Bistro 4), La Cabane and Casa Del Popolo the hosting places for pre-existing scenes, spaces productive of their own scenes, moments in the itinerary of a scene (in the course of a night, or over many years), local examples of scenic phenomena whose true scale is international, or points within networks of social, cultural, and economic interconnection which are themselves the real scenes?" He references the St-Laurent watering hole La Cabane as a meeting place for his peers in the academic/art/journalism scene of the 1980s. He notes that if it were to close the participants would no longer gather—meaning the venue is the cornerstone of the scene itself.

Bohemia, the word and the way of life, was imported into North America in 1853 by Henry Clapp Jr., the son of a devout family from Nantucket. He developed a career in journalism and travelled to Paris in 1849 to attend a three-day world peace congress. He stayed three years. Clapp settled in the heart of the Latin Quarter, still very poor and filled with students. The teetotaling Clapp discovered the cafés and learned to speak French perfectly. He even began to drink. Although bohemianism had by this time become a way of life in Paris, in 1849, three months after Clapp arrived, the city went wild over an unusual play based on sketches written by Henry Murger called *Scènes de la Bohème*. Destitute, Murger had been living in the area, frequenting the Café Momus with other penniless writers and artists such as Charles Baudelaire. Théodore Barrière transformed these stories of Murger's circle of bohemians into the play *La vie de Bohème*. It was a smashing success and the talk of the town. As Justin Martin writes in his account of the time *Rebel Souls*: "The play succeeded as nothing had before in defining its myriad compass points: intense passion for art; more talk of art than actual making of art; cafés, strong coffee, stronger alcohol; a near pathological fear of conventionality and a charming insouciance in the face of impending disaster; no money; no prospects, no qualms about romance, and most vividly, early tragic death, often hastened by damp, chilly garret conditions." Clapp soaked up the mania over the play and lived the lifestyle. Upon returning to the US, he chose New York for his experiment, to recreate the bohemia of Paris. He just needed a venue.

In 1856, he found Pfaff's Restaurant and Saloon on Broadway at Bleeker and settled into the basement. Broadway was a wide street where many people would stroll due to the lack of parks in the city at the time. Clapp had found his Café Momus. Now he needed to find some bohemians. Here is where his personality as organizer and public speaker took hold, and soon there was a group of eclectic artists frequenting Pfaff's who became known as the Pfaff Bohemians. There was the writer Fitz-James O'Brien, immensely talented but a brawler, alcoholic, and lacking motivation. The famous political cartoonist Thomas Nast showed up as a teenager. Artemus Ward was America's first stand-up comedian and an influence on Mark Twain. The Queen of Bohemia was the writer and single parent Ada Clare. Fitz Hugh Ludlow was a psychedelic pioneer and the author of the literary sensation *The Hashish Eater*. Edwin Booth came from a family of dramatic actors and his brother John Wilkes Booth eventually shot President Lincoln at Ford's Theatre. Adah Menken was a performer, the Marilyn Monroe of her time. And the most famous of all was Walt Whitman, who entered Pfaff's in 1858, having walked over the bridge from Brooklyn. He frequented the saloon almost every day but was also slightly outside the scene, since half of the venue was used as a gay bar, and he was interested in exploring both sides of his personality. Although critics don't write much about this period in Whitman's life, his visits to Pfaff's and the bohemian crowd obviously influenced his poetry. He had published the first two editions of *Leaves of Grass* before meeting the Pfaff Bohemians but, in 1860 he published a vastly expanded edition, featuring more than one hundred new poems, including a new section devoted to love among men, the permissive atmosphere of Pfaff's allowing Whitman (who still lived with his mother) to open up and be his authentic self.

Clapp had assembled his eccentrics and began to publish a journal called *The Saturday Press* in 1858. It was short-lived but was one of the most influential publications in America, achieving a moment of cultural zeitgeist for the Pfaff Bohemians and rescuing Whitman from obscurity. The group disbanded at the beginning of the American Civil War, a time of immense disruption and chaos. As Martin explains, due to the fact that some of the Pfaff crowd became war correspondents, the term *bohemian* became synonymous with *journalist* for a time (scruffy hard-drinking writers), before fading out of usage.

The bohemian scene in Paris continued in the Belle Epoque of the 1880s in the Montmartre neighbourhood. At Le Chat Noir were featured the shadow-plays of Henri-Rivière. But one of the best-known bohemians to come out of France at this time was the painter Henri de Toulouse-Lautrec. Born with a crippling form of hereditary dwarfism, he was raised in an affluent family and tried to enter the official art schools for painting. This path proved frustrating. He discovered his authentic self when he moved into the neighbourhood of Montmartre—at the time still a rural enclave, not even a part of the city. He drank excessively, painted portraits of prostitutes, hung out at the cabarets and dancehalls of the area, especially the Moulin Rouge, and caroused with Vincent van Gogh before his untimely death. He shot to fame in 1891, much to the horror of his family, when he lithographed the poster *Moulin Rouge, La Goulue*, which featured a dancer in a provocative pose. He became known more for these posters, which in hindsight defined the neighbourhood and the spirit of the times, than for his paintings. He died from a combination of alcoholism and syphilis at the age of thirty-six.

The Dada movement was also centered around a venue and was active in publishing what have been called the first art zines. Hugo Ball, a German poet and playwright, exiled in neutral Switzerland, advertised The Cabaret Voltaire in the Zurich press in February, 1916. It was to be a group of young artists and writers forming with the objective of becoming a centre for artistic entertainment in reaction to the insanity of the war. The cabaret was inaugurated three days later in the back room of the Holländische Meierei, a popular tavern located in a seedy section of Zurich. Jan Ephraïm, the owner of the establishment, turned the job of emcee over to Ball with the hope of attracting a large audience. Ball took as his model the Parisian cabaret tradition, born with Le Chat Noir in 1881, which he associated with the cabaret spirit that had existed in Berlin before the war. Refugee artists from all over Europe quickly besieged the scene at the establishment. It lasted four months before poet Tristan Tzara performed his "Dada Manifesto" and created the publication *Dada*. Other members were painter Marcel Janco, artist Hans Arp, Richard Huelsenbeck, and Sophie Taeuber. The art and design created by these artists included readymades (made famous by Marcel Duchamp in New York) and collage. Other Dada periodicals were *Dada Jazz, Mécano, 75HP, Merz, New York*

Dada, and *Cabaret Voltaire*. The importance of the Dada movement to the underground press is made evident in the fact that Liz Worth gives a history of Dadaism and DIY art in issue #10 of *Fish Piss*: "If you heard about a nihilistic movement that was centered around anti-aesthetic creations, disgust over bourgeois values, and protest activities, you might think someone was talking about your plans for the weekend.... When comparing Dada and the DIY ethics of fringe cultures of today, much of the artwork itself is comparable, especially when looking at early punk albums and zines."

Emily Hahn in her book *Dada Magazines* makes the case explicit that it was the journals and (maga)zines) produced by the members of the Dada movement that not only *defined* Dada itself, but also acted to spread the word of Dada to other cities and artistic communities at a time when the people themselves could not cross borders due to the war: "Diasporic from the start, Dada's distinctly networked and transnational nature would not have been possible without the journals." Hahn writes: "The magazines made Dada what it was, something that becomes evident when we recognize them as active agents within the movement. More than simply neutral ferries carrying reproductions from one place to another, Dada periodicals were active, creative venues." Here the link is made between a periodical and a venue, and later in her book Hahn calls them a "meeting place" or "creative exhibition venues." As with *Fish Piss*, the pages of the zine acted as the *space* for the contributors to define their own community. "The journals not only broadcast the group as an established collective; they effectively made it so by displaying their works and giving them a name; Dadaists, like others before them and since, understood the printed medium as a requisite part of establishing a movement." Because they treated the journals as works of art in themselves, the Dadaists began to experiment with page layout and therefore the journals play an important role in the history of graphic design. Their use of typography was innovative and "sabotaged legibility, a provocative, political gesture at a time of fervent attempts to streamline communication technologies, which had become weaponized in this first mechanized war."

The continued influence of Dada periodicals on zines is made clear in Hahn's closing chapter, which features a Bay Area mail art group, with links to Fluxus, who made "Dadazines" in the 1970s. These were "amateur, small-circulation publications," such as *West Bay Dadaist* and *New York Correspondence School Weekly Breeder*, "which merge past and present by combining excerpts from reproductions of Dada journals and 1970s newspapers and magazines," a cut-and-paste strategy reaching across time. These zinesters and many since (including Rastelli), adopted Dada techniques by drawing on "Dada's resistance to the art market; manipulation of language; transnational reach; subversive, sardonic sense of humour; collage techniques; self-publishing; and dependence on the postal system."

Dada ended in Zurich when the war ended and exiled

artists returned home. The Dada movement expanded to cities across Europe and New York but never with the centrality of the scene around the cabaret in Zurich. Publications like *Dada* defined a community in much the same way *Fish Piss* defined a bohemia. Dada was over by 1922 when André Breton created Surrealism. Obviously, the Dada spirit lives on.

Montreal in the 1990s was probably closest in aesthetic to the Paris Left Bank of 1920-1928, with writers and artists living in an affordable part of town, but importantly, as language exiles. As Gen from Derivative Records and Pest 5000 put it at the time: "Montreal's like that expatriate community in Paris between the wars. The kind of sense of moving to a place which is cheap, where you don't necessarily speak the language, which is somewhat depressed, not only economically, but also in spirit and beautiful in its decrepitude." The difference would be in post-WWI America there was a definite movement to discover the bohemia of Paris due to its thriving history. It was a destination. Whereas, in Montreal we were there by default. We were what remained after the Referendum, it was an anti-destination. Humphrey Carpenter in *Geniuses Together*, writes that the "idea" of Greenwich Village had lost its appeal by 1920, and "it was fast becoming—in a diluted version — the lifestyle of the middle classes" which coincided with the rise of the "idea" of the bohemian, "which had become a fashionable word. Wives of businessmen in Milwaukee patronized 'bohemian' antique shops, browsed in little 'bohemian' bookstores, and gave 'bohemian' parties." The exchange rate all over Europe after the war certainly helped, and of course escaping Prohibition was very appealing to many.

Sylvia Beach and her bookstore Shakespeare and Company was a central node, especially since she offered a lending library to those who could not pay. Her biggest contribution to literary history was offering to publish the novel *Ulysses*, which *The Little Review* had ceased publishing due to obscenity charges. Author James Joyce made her life a living hell with hundreds of last-minute revisions on the proofs, which extended the book and the print job until it was out of control. A young Ernest Hemingway showed up at the bookshop in 1921 with a letter of introduction from Sherwood Anderson, after being wounded as an ambulance driver in the war. He was able to supplement his income by writing European reports for the *Toronto Star,* which allowed him to travel to places like Spain where his first novel *The Sun Also Rises* takes place. The original title for this book was *The Lost Generation*, which is what Gertude Stein had called the Americans in Paris at the time. She hosted a weekly salon in her Latin Quarter apartment, where Picassos decorated the walls. The Americans all congregated together as a group and took over the Dome and Rotonde in the neighbourhood of Montparnasse, prompting some like Hemingway to find new cafés, away from them. Marcel Duchamp commented that the neighbourhood was superior to Montmartre, Greenwich Village, or Chelsea because unlike them, it was not populated by art students but was full of established painters and so seemed more mature. However, "the presence of the French painters and writers soon attracted Americans to Montparnasse, and the Americans attracted more Americans. In the early 1920s the plain little cafés and bistros began to disappear from the Boulevard du Montparnasse and its side streets, to be replaced by more ambitious establishments competing for the new arrival's money." Some Americans realized the European Dream was just as false as the American one.

Hemingway's wife Hadley paid most of the bills and took care of their baby so he concentrated on developing a new sparse way of writing. In his memoir of the time, *A Moveable Feast*, he explained cryptically, "All you have to do is write one true sentence." He also describes going on a ski trip to Switzerland when they run out of money and leaving the cat to babysit! After meeting Ford Madox Ford, Hemingway began to edit the *transatlantic review* and included a few of his own stories, eventually published as *In Our Time*. He serialized Gertrude Stein's *The Making of Americans* and published excerpts from Joyce's next work in progress, eventually titled *Finnegan's Wake*. F. Scott Fitzgerald was impressed enough with Hemingway to introduce him to his editor at Scribners but the feeling was not mutual. Fitzgerald had a hit at twenty-four-years-old with *This Side of Paradise* but was insecure around the tough guy Hemingway. Somewhere between the Deux Magots and Lipps bar, he managed to write his masterpiece

The Great Gatsby. The community of writers in English was so large that small English language publishers sprang up to print their writing—works that the London or NY companies would not touch, often regretfully, in hindsight. Aside from Sylvia Beach, there was Robert McAlmon's Contact Publishing, Bill Bird and the Three Mountains, Stein's Plain Editions, and Harry and Caresse Crosby's The Black Sun. There were many other expatriate writers and painters in Paris at this time, including John Glasso from Montreal and Morley Callaghan from Toronto. Most of them wrote memoirs of their time there. The ones that stayed seemed to be the ones that focused on their craft and integrated into the French community, like Hemingway escaping the cafés filled with Americans. In other words, the authentic bohemians.

Kiki of Montparnasse is the perfect example of the authentic bohemian paradigm. Beginning with her name change (in the same way that Jack Dylan changed his name to denote his entry to bohemia) from Alice Ernestine Prin, she grew up poor on the outskirts of Paris. She became a model, muse, and cabaret singer/performer at such cafés as the Café de la Rotonde, where artists went looking for models and models for artists. Kiki recognized that the cafés were where you went to change your life, that there was power in an alias, especially for women after the war. In 1921, she could be found on the street hawking the slim arts-and-letters review *Montparnasse* for a few extra sous. She met and fell in love with the American avant-garde photographer Man Ray who had changed his name for completely different reasons: he was a Jewish immigrant hoping to avoid rising antisemitism. She became his creative partner and muse, and she used her influence as an insider to help him become famous. She even used the name "Kiki Ray" when acting in one of his films.

The Bloomsbury group in England has often been referred to as bohemian, and there are a number of good reasons for this. Their group included writers, painters, and publishers, even an economist: Lytton Strachey, Dora Carrington, Duncan Grant, E.M. Forster, and Maynard Keynes. The most famous member was the Modernist writer Virginia Woolf, who together with her husband Leonard Woolf bought a printing press and formed The Hogarth Press in 1915 to print her first books without censor, which they disseminated by hand. In this way, they were no different than zinesters doing it for themselves. Their symbolic capital drew writers such as T.S. Eliot and Katherine Mansfield to the press. The group were centralized in the neighbourhood of London from which it took its name. However, I believe the difference between the Bloomsbury crowd and "authentic" bohemians was one of class. The group initially formed around a society called the Apostles at Cambridge University, an aristocratic institution. Although Woolf was writing novels against the grain of the establishment (such as *To the Lighthouse* in 1925 or the feminist classic *A Room of One's Own* in 1929), she was also mostly known at the time for writing criticism for the *London Times Literary Supplement*, definitely an establishment newspaper. Leonard was a former civil servant and editor at *The Nation*. The central venue for their meetings was the country cottage they owned, Monk's House. In fact, Woolf's lover Vita Sackville-West was raised in a palace! The fact that the Woolf's owned a country house and a place in the city at 52 Tavistock Square, complete with servants, makes one question their bohemian credentials. Bohemians do not have cooks and gardeners on the payroll. Or as Alison Light puts it: "Virginia's dependence on her servants plays havoc with any easy celebration of either her or her sister, the painter Vanessa Bell, as bohemian, free women, creating a new kind of life. The servants don't usually feature in accounts of 'Bloomsbury's women.'"

Back in a liberated Paris after the Second World War, a group was gathering which would come to define a whole movement in literature and philosophy, one called Existentialism. In the neighbourhood of Saint-Germaine-des-Près, where you could get a cheap room with a bed and a basin and little else, Jean-Paul Sartre and feminist icon Simone de Beauvoir sipped coffee and scribbled notes at the Café Flore. Jean Genet and Albert Camus frequented the cafe as well. At night, jazz cellars like the Tabou were filled with patrons dressed in black. In 1945, Sartre launched a cultural journal called *Les Temps modernes* whose editorial board included many regulars from the Flore. There was a flurry of writing after the liberation of Paris, and Sartre argued for writers to be active and committed, for a *littérature engagée.* There was so much writing, produced so quickly, that they needed a publication to contain it all. The title comes from the 1936 film *Modern Times* starring Charlie Chaplin, which was influential to Sartre and de Beauvoir. According to Sarah Bakewell in her book *At the Existentialist Café*, "*Les Temps modernes* became one of the great engines of intellectual debate in France and beyond." Impressive legacy for a zine.

A number of African Americans such as James Baldwin, Langston Hughes, and Richard Wright left the Harlem Renaissance for the more tolerant race relations of Paris and fit into this crowd of like-minded intellectuals. In fact, James Baldwin wrote his first novel, *Go Tell it on the Mountain*, at the Café Flore, though in his essay, "Equal in Paris," he suggests that the bohemian scene made it difficult to write: "The moment I began living in French hotels, I understood the necessity of French cafés. This made it rather difficult to look me up, for as soon as I was out of bed, I hopefully took notebook and fountain pen off to the upstairs room of the Flore, where I consumed rather a lot of coffee and, as evening approached, rather a lot of alcohol, but did not get much writing done." In the late 1950s, the Beats would live in the neighbourhood. Ginsberg, Corso, and Orlovsky lived at the Hotel Rachou, dubbed "the Beat Hotel." William S. Burroughs joined them in 1959, and local editor Maurice Girodias published *Naked Lunch* through his Olympia Press, notorious for publishing low-grade pornography in English for the consumption of foreign tourists, who because of censorship could not obtain such materials at home. (French censorship laws had a loophole allowing English works to be published without domestic confiscation). But occasionally Girodias achieved spectacular literary coups, Vladimir Nabakov's *Lolita* and Samuel Beckett's Malone trilogy to give other examples.

The name and location of Greenwich Village in New York has always been synonymous with bohemia. The village became "The Village" on an evening in 1917 when Marcel Duchamp and friends climbed to the top of the Washington Square arch and declared it "a free and independent republic." Before this, the area was "the only community in America where Edgar Allan Poe could score drugs in the 1840s and Henry James could stroll past grazing cows in the 1890s," according to Ross Wetzsteon in his book *Republic of Dreams*. Other prominent residents before 1917 were Herman Melville and Mark Twain. A few blocks away at 23 Fifth Avenue, Mabel Dodge, influenced by her friend Gertrude Stein, opened a successful salon that introduced the locals (sometimes one hundred at a time) to Freud, birth control, and the Wobblies. Some of the guests might include photographer Alfred Stieglitz and anarchist Emma Goldman. In 1913, Dodge served as one of the sponsors of the famous Armory Show, which introduced cubism to America. She acted as the conduit for the Village radicals. Dodge's salon drew criticism however, and her group of bohemians were accused of only "talking about talking and thinking about thinking."

Max Eastman took over the editorship of the socialist magazine *The Masses* in 1912, and became "one of the most famous radicals in America." The staff member who brought him in was the cartoonist Art Young. The magazine had folded since no one was willing to take control of a "co-operative" enterprise. It was Eastman who navigated the politics, fundraising, and responsibility. Interestingly, what drew him to take the position was the same thing that draws zine makers to make a zine: "Combining the infantile delight of cutting out paper dolls... with the adult satisfaction of fooling yourself into thinking you are molding public opinion." And his comments to his detractors sound eerily familiar: "*The Masses* exists to publish what commercial magazines will not pay for and will not publish." The list of writers and artists that contributed to the magazine over its five-year run is staggering: Sherwood Anderson, Upton Sinclair, Djuna Barnes, William Carlos Williams, Amy Lowell, Bertrand Russell, and even Pablo Picasso to name but a few. To be published in *The Masses* "became a badge of acceptance in the radical community, worth more to these idealistic rebels than any amount of money." Polly's restaurant and the Liberal Club was their bohemian node.

The Liberal Club was also the gathering venue for a secret club of women artists and intellectuals who sparked what would become modern feminism. It was often women who were the hosts or nodal points of the bohemian "salon" scenes: Gertude Stein in Paris or Mabel Dodge in Greenwich Village are but two examples. Traditionally, the salon was a "safe space" for women to get the education denied them in traditional scholastic institutions. The Heterodoxy Club was founded by Marie Jenney Howe in 1912 and began as a way for women to fight for the right to vote. Their members were writers and actresses, teachers, lawyers, socialites, and socialists. These were women outside the mainstream, many of them divorced—at the time of a 2% divorce rate—or openly lesbian. They were educated, outspoken activists, but they also had to be independently wealthy with leisure time and a desire to pay the dues, which meant white, middle-class and Protestant. Regardless, they helped define the term *feminist*. In her book *Hotbed*, Joanna Scutts describes their venue: "In a place that feels, just then, like the brightly pulsing centre of the universe, a group of women gathers to talk about the world, and their place in it." They have gathered at a townhouse on MacDougal Street in the heart of the Village. Upstairs is the Liberal Club which bills itself as "A Social Center for Those Interested in New Ideas" and next door is the Washington Square Bookshop. "The Village isn't a tourist attraction, at least not yet—it's a place to live, to be, to *become*." Downstairs in the basement is a restaurant known as Polly's where "the whole point is to overhear your neighbours' conversations, lean over, and join in. It's what makes the Village the Village."

When physician and poet William Carlos Williams travelled from New Jersey to see the Armory Show of 1913, he was delighted because "the exhibition represented in painting what he was hoping to achieve in writing." He began to frequent the studios of the Village and counted the painters living there as his closest friends. Soon he was helping put together one of the little magazines of the time called *Others*, which featured his poetry next to that of Ezra Pound, Wallace Stevens, and T.S. Eliot. After WWI, the successful poetry magazine *The Dial* began to minimize politics and publish more poetry, and by 1922 the circulation was an impressive fourteen thousand. Said one editor, "*The Dial* made a noise in the world… It directly affected the artistic life of a generation, and indirectly the life of our whole time." The editorship was taken over by William's friend Marianne Moore in 1925. Thomas Wolfe wrote his novel *Look Homeward, Angel* (1929) in a rundown Village apartment. Later, the Abstract Expressionists, including Jackson Pollock, created "a new image of the painter in the American imagination" as "an unstable mixture of the romantic and the apocalyptic resulting from a combination of self-dramatization and media myth." Their venue of choice was a bar called The Cedar, "the cathedral of American culture in the fifties." In other words, they were continuing the neighbourhood tradition of bohemia.

The fifties welcomed the Beats to the neighbourhood, to bars like the San Remo, sometimes called the "American Café de Flore" and the White Horse Tavern where Dylan Thomas and Norman Mailer were also frequent imbibers. Mailer was approached by the editor of *Esquire* in The

Five Spot at a Thelonious Monk concert to write a piece of political journalism, which began his reputation as an "unorthodox polemicist." In his infamous essay about bohemianism called "The White Negro," he introduced the "existentialist hipster hero, living outside the normal constraints of society in order to avoid annihilation by social conformity, abiding by the code of the Negro," which presumably meant smoking marijuana, listening to jazz, and getting into violent skirmishes. Obviously, this position was controversial/racist even at the time, but it turned Mailer into a "public intellectual" on top of his fame as a novelist. However, Mailer was able to get at a nugget of truth, "that hipsterdom is all about chasing after Blackness, and is inevitably just as vague, extractive, and racist as that sounds." In *Hip: The History,* John Leland writes extensively about the Beats as naïve hipsters who "made a fetish of Black disenfranchisement." The Beats "romanticized Black life at the margins, imagining it as spontaneous and uncorrupted, liberated from both the war legacy and the economy. It was their ticket away from the centre." In 1958, with the royalties from his successful books *The Naked and the Dead* and *The Deer Park,* Mailer co-founded an alternative newspaper called *The Village Voice,* arguably the template for the alt-weekly papers which proliferated during the 1990s, including the *Montreal Mirror* and *Hour* in Montreal.

The *Evergreen Review* (1957-1966) was formed in the Village and helped define the "Beat Generation," a label coined by John Clellon Holmes, the author of the novel

Go, in a *New York Times* magazine article. Edited by Barney Rosset, *The Evergreen Review* published Beat writers Allen Ginsberg, Jack Kerouac, Gregory Corso, and William S. Burroughs alongside international writers and those from the Literature of the Absurd, such as Samuel Beckett and Eugène Ionesco. It brought the two strands of post-war writing together. It also was the first to identify the Beats as part of the San Francisco Scene. Allen Ginsberg famously first read his poem "Howl" at Six Gallery in San Francisco on October 7, 1955, and the published version was one of the first in the Pocket Poets Series from Lawrence Ferlinghetti's City Lights Books, for which he faced an obscenity trial. "Howl" was to become the calling card of the new movement in literature.

The Beats did produce zines, but not surprisingly, it was two poets from marginalized groups who stepped up to represent in the DIY medium. Together with Hettie Jones, African American LeRoi Jones (later Amiri Baraka) founded *Yugen*, a poetry journal designed with a Zen aesthetic to compete with other small press anthologies, but for the off-Beats. It brought together the Beats, the Black Mountain Poets, and the New York School poets of the late 1950s. Hettie Jones had previously worked at *Partisan Review* and used her background and knowledge (especially in design) to give *Yugen* an air of respectability and professionalism.

The other publication was *Floating Bear* which was a mimeographed zine of poetry edited by Diane di Prima, who used it as a community bulletin board for Beat poetry.

It was only sold by subscription to a few hundred poets in the know who "jammed" on its pages. It was distributed through the postal service semi-monthly, but its influence far outweighed its print run, and it helped to define a community. Di Prima had cut her teeth with *Yugen* between 1958-62 and worked with Jones on the first twenty-five issues of *Floating Bear*. As a woman in the 1950s, di Prima must have felt making a zine was a way of subverting the male-dominated Beat Generation. She did it for herself, but also, by making it an anthology and by subscription, she democratically brought the community together. As Brown puts it, "Not only was di Prima creating a new space for which unpublished, ignored, or new writers could share their work publicly, the medium through which she was able to circulate this information was self-made and self-directed."

The Village was the closest thing the Beats had to a home base. Burroughs released *Junky* in 1953 as an Ace paperback, intended to be sold to subway riders, about his experiences as a drug addict, "lush roller" and small-time Greenwich Village heroin pusher. Displaced French Canadian Jack Kerouac and Allen Ginsberg had attended the neighbouring Columbia University, and Gregory Corso was born in the Village. Kerouac wrote the seminal novel of the times *On the Road*, about his adventures criss-crossing the country, in 1951, but it wasn't published until 1957, when a *New York Times* review made him a star and a spokesman for his generation literally overnight. In the frenzy that followed, "Beatnik" replaced "Bohemian" in the cultural lexicon, complete with parodies of bongo-playing, beret-toting, goateed poets. But the real Beats were nothing like the parody. As Ned Polsky writes in his sociological examination of 1960, *Hustlers, Beats, and Others*:

> Until recently the term 'hipster' meant simply one who is hip, roughly the equivalent of a beat. Beats recognized that the hipster is more of an 'operator'—has a more consciously patterned life-style (such as a concern to dress well) and makes more frequent economic raids on the frontiers of the square world—but emphasized their social bonds with hipsters, such as their liking for drugs, for jazz music, and, above all, their common scorn for bourgeois career orientations... In their own eyes beats are hip, but they are definitely not hipsters.

This might be a good time to examine the concept of "hip," a bohemian-adjacent socio-cultural descriptor. Although many of the signature elements exist in both groups, bohemians originated in Europe and hip is a decidedly American phenomenon. In his book *Hip: The History*, John Leland writes: "Hip is not simply the sum of What's Hot Now. In a country that resisted the class hierarchies of Europe, hip offers an alternative status system, independent of money or bloodline." But mostly what separates them is that hip has everything to do with the unique structure of slavery in

American history: "What distinguished the United States is both simple and, in its ramifications, maddeningly, insolubly complex. That difference is the presence of Africans, and the coexistence of two very different populations in a new country with undefined boundaries. Without the Africans, there is no hip."

The original hipsters were African American bebop aficionados in the 1950s who revered a complex form of jazz they assumed was outside the white mainstream, but the term eventually attached itself to white people imitating Black people. However, it was the "blackface minstrel show, which hit the American stage in the 1820s and 1830s, that was the purest projection of this ambivalence. Minstrelsy provided a model for white curiosity and co-option of Black forms, a superstructure of hip." Enslaved people used a guarded method of talking around their owners in order not to be understood by them. This "Black English" became a type of hip talk which was intended to be opaque but became richly ambiguous. Using this language and its cultural codes, a modern urban white person can become codified as hip, colonizing marginal neighbourhoods and accessing popular culture which they couldn't through other means. "If hip is an awareness, the new cities provided tight clusters of like minds to circulate its codes, defining themselves in the process." Although often associated with musical taste, being hip rarely involves the production of a small publication, or the production of any artistic activity for that matter, and in that way differs from being a bohemian.

Former football player Jack Kerouac had written many unpublished works while waiting for his big break, so when it came, the books were released one at a time to take advantage of his fame. His novel *The Subterraneans*, about a mixed-race relationship with Mardou Fox and the underground community of jazz-loving white bohemians in San Francisco, is so poorly written and cringe-worthy to modern sensibilities, it is no wonder it went unpublished. Here is how Kerouac describes the patrons at a local bar: "They are hip without being slick, intelligent without being corny, they are intellectual as hell and know all about Pound without being pretentious... they are very Christlike." Jazz was the music of the Beats, who embraced bebop and the new forms of music coming from musicians like Charlie Parker and Thelonious Monk. In this sense, they were the cliché of hip. The Beats became the rebellious freewheeling, drug smoking, anti-establishment mentors for the counterculture of the 1960s. Bob Dylan even took Allen Ginsberg on tour with him after he broke out of the Greenwich Village coffeehouses on MacDougall Street.

And how has Canada fared in the realm of bohemia? The main candidate would be the community surrounding the Yorkville neighbourhood in downtown Toronto in the 1960s. As Stuart Henderson recounts in *Making the Scene*:

> In Canada no scene grew to match the proportions (real or mythical) of Toronto's Yorkville. A budding

> multi-cultural metropolis, straddling a staid, puritanical past, and a complex, immigration-fueled future, Toronto would play reluctant host to what was widely perceived to be the centre of the hip world in the 1960s.

But it was all over by 1970, and the district would become unrecognizable with the glitz and glamour of today. A timeline of the neighbourhood as a bohemian zone would begin in 1960 with the flight to the suburbs of the middle class and an occupation of the older Victorian row houses by European immigrants. These outsiders brought European café culture to the area and opened a number of coffeeshops. These sorts of euro-cafés did not exist previously in Toronto, and since the drinking age was twenty-one the coffeehouses attracted the youth to the area. Quickly, the "Village," as it was becoming known, transitioned from a quiet ethnic neighbourhood to a "lively bohemian haunt," as Henderson describes it. Venues opened and became central locus points of hip, such as The Gaslight, The Purple Onion, The Half Beat, and 71. A small group of writers, actors, and folk singers occupied these spaces which became "a community of clubhouses." Ian Tyson, also very influenced by the Beats down south, was one of these folksingers, who claimed the coffeehouses were "sprouting like mushrooms." Indeed, by 1965 their number in the neighbourhood peaked at twenty-two. Other musicians who would later come out of this music scene were Neil Young, Joni Mitchell, Gordon Lightfoot, and Bruce Cockburn. The Bohemian Embassy opened to promote more eclectic entertainment—featuring singers, writers, painters, and comedians. At this venue writers such as Margaret Atwood, Earle Birney, and Gwendolyn MacEwen would get their start. The Mousetrap was a pioneering venture in that it provided gay youth with a safe hub for their own bohemia.

The publication which represented the Yorkville scene was *Harbinger*, produced out of the Golden Ant, one of the city's first health food stores, co-owned and co-edited by Hans Wetzel and David Bush. Founded in April, 1968, at first the anti-establishment zine was "long on enthusiasm and short on cash" and featured a "chaotic potpourri of obscure personal opinions and sometimes meaningless banter from one drug-induced vision or another." The publication was read by students and in turn covered the happenings at the controversial alternative college Rochdale, which came to epitomize the counterculture in Toronto, an "intellectual maelstrom" which the paper only too willingly embraced. In November, 1969, the cover bore a controversial drawing by Roger Greco of a naked woman giving birth, and *Harbinger* became infamous overnight. The editors were arrested on obscenity charges. At their trial, the judge determined that the publication met the definition of obscene and the editors were found guilty and fined harshly. Of course, in the spirit of the times, *Harbinger* went on to satirize the trial in its own pages.

The peak of the Village scene was from 1964-66, but it was quickly discovered "by mass media, local teenagers, and the wider university-aged community. With the scene expanding every weekend, Yorkville went from being a mere cultural curiosity, an enclave defined by Euro-chic shopping by day and bohemians by night, to a thronging, intensely crowded party zone." Of course, this created problems. Interestingly enough, the conflict that followed paints a portrait of the difference between the black-clad bohemian aesthetic, passed on from the Beats, and the rising hippie aesthetic, adopted by the huge influx of bored youth: "The early associations with the coffeehouse bohemia were disappearing from Yorkville, only to be replaced by younger, more raucous, volatile, and apparently less artsy connotations." The watershed year for Yorkville was 1967:

> Defined by an ever-expanding population of runaways, drop-outs, activists, drug users, emerging rock stars, bikers, and peace-and-lovers, Yorkville's summer of love was fractious, exciting, and often dramatic. This was the year Yorkville became unavoidably politicized, a self-conscious cultural battleground over which various factions clamoured for control, arguing over the elusive mantle of authentic Village identity.

Finally, by 1970 all the bohemians had fled the neighbourhood, abandoning the place to the paranoid drug addicts and undercover cops. Developers moved in, and by the mid-seventies the area was transformed into a high-end boutique district.

Hippies were not bohemians. They did not operate outside the dominant culture but, as Henderson says of the Yorkville Village participants, "In his or her rejection of this dominant culture, the hippie is in fact operating from within, *not without*, the same culture." They represented an entire counterculture, and their very mass disqualified them from bohemia. Michael Harrington in 1972 wrote that "a bohemia that enrolls a good portion of a generation is no longer a bohemia" because the scope of bohemia needs to be intimate and organized on a human, or neighbourhood-based, scale. It's common for the term "The Village" to substitute for "bohemia" in some cases. "The clothes, the hostility to middle-class values, were very much like those of bohemia. But they were a mass movement on an unchartered social frontier." The counterculture was so large and all-pervasive that it became the mainstream culture, as proven by the music from the bands quickly becoming the popular music of the time. "The Village was large enough to have a sense of community, of society, and small enough for everyone to remain an individual. It is something else again—and not bohemia—when hundreds of thousands gather at Woodstock Festival to listen to the highly paid superstars in commercialized and collectivized rites of liberation." To be a bohemian, one needs to be invested in intellectual pursuits in small groups, but hippies for the most part wanted to gather in large groups to protest the war and drop out and get stoned. Once the US pulled out of Vietnam, there was nothing to protest and the hippies returned to their middle-class lives, propelling the future corporate culture of the 1980s.

When not sleeping on Kits Beach, the hippy community in Vancouver, which centered around Gastown, was a mellower version of San Francisco's Haight-Ashbury. It was complete with its own alternative press publication, *The Georgia Straight* and the cartoonist Rand Holmes at the centre of the scene. Holmes was an Edmonton expat who quickly established himself with comics about a character named Harold Hedd, who resembled Gilbert Shelton's *Fabulous Furry Freak Brothers*. But Harold was genderqueer and once appeared on the cover of the paper snorting cocaine off another man's penis. His comics were the most popular feature in the newspaper by far. In 1971, police officers rounded up anyone in Gastown who looked like a hippy. Two writers from *The Georgia Straight* arranged a marijuana "smoke-in and street jamboree" to take place at Maple Tree Square in Gastown. That evening, an estimated two thousand people showed up to protest Operation Dustpan. On the evening of August 7, 1971, after years of mounting tension, it finally snapped. The result was one of Vancouver's most infamous and bloody riots. In the 1980s, *The Georgia Straight* became just another alternative weekly, the sort of media zines were designed to counterbalance.

Also in Vancouver was the poetry group TISH which came out of the Creative Writing program at UBC in 1960. They were not relegated to a certain venue or part of the city; in fact, much of their lifestyle was defined by driving cars. Frank Davey put out nineteen issues of a mimeograph zine called *TISH* and attended regular basement gatherings held at the home of one of the professors, Warren Tallman, on West 37th, in the well-to-do Kerrisdale neighbourhood. Tallman invited Beat poets Allen Ginsberg and Robert Duncan to read at UBC, which influenced the group, including Fred Wah, Daphne Marlatt, and George Bowering. Were the TISH members bohemians? One would be tempted to say they were a distant cousin of the Beats and certainly shared a belief in breaking apart the traditional poetic discourse, but due to the lack of centralized community outside academia, they were probably not bohemians in the true sense. Also, bohemians don't drive.

But what about a precedent in Montreal for bohemia? The Sin City of the forties and fifties can be considered a form of bohemia, but it was more about illegal versus alternative culture. The economic paradigm was skewed due to so much of the operation being run by the mob. An interesting case for bohemia could be made for the Vehicule Poets of the 1970s which sprung from a group of artists working out of Véhicule Art Inc.—situated on Ste-Catherine Street West near St-Laurent Boulevard—

one of Canada's first artist-run galleries. The large space occupied by both the gallery and the print shop that became Véhicule Press was once the Café Montmartre—a renowned jazz club of the 1930s. The non-profit artist-run gallery was created to provide a venue for experimental local and international artists, and a space for dance, performance, music, and regular poetry readings. This meets the criteria for bohemia of a centralized venue.

According to Simon Dardick, a member of the press that was situated at the back of the gallery, "in addition to publishing poetry, we collaborated with member artists of the gallery such as Suzy Lake, Bill Vazan, Allan Bealy, and Frank Vitale, to create unique artists' books and magazines. It was a period of exciting cross-fertilization between writers and visual artists." Dardick and his wife Nancy Marrelli continue to run Véhicule Press out of the Plateau neighbourhood to this day.

Leonard Cohen and Irving Layton had dominated the poetry community of Montreal throughout the 1960s, but when they left, there was a gap. The Vehicule Poets were interested in the intersection of art, poetry, and performance, and were schooled in the history of Dada. (For reasons unclear, the group did not employ the accent in their name). Ken Norris joined the group in 1975:

> The Vehicule Poets were something of a poetry band. Not too much of that stuff wound up in

print, but there were numerous performances of really odd texts. We were bringing Dada and Surrealism to Montreal, which really needed some loosening up at the time.... We were actively cultivating a conscious radicalism. We went out of our way to be agent provocateurs.

Norris also points out the connection to the TISH poets since George Bowering was teaching at Concordia at the time and the first book by the press to obtain Canada Council funding was Bowering's jab at Montreal, *The Concrete Island: Montreal Poems 1967-71*. Another member, poet Endre Farkas describes the scene by saying:

Since nobody really knew what they were doing, you were free to do whatever you wanted.... One of the things that happened in the sixties and seventies was that the artists actually started to use the media, as opposed to just listening to it. You now control, as opposed to it controlling you.

The regular Sunday night readings at the gallery formalized the group by 1977. Other members of the Vehicule Poets were Tom Konyves, Claudia Lapp, Artie Gold, John McAuley, and Stephen Morrissey.

Arguably, the next generation poetry venue was Bistro 4 located at the intersection of St-Laurent Boulevard and Duluth, in the heart of the Plateau. Although most of the performers had no idea who the Vehicule Poets were, there was still the sense of "actively cultivating a conscious radicalism" especially in the two main reading series that happened there, YAWP! and Enough Said. Bistro 4 was beginning to be known as a venue hosting various shows and launches including A Moveable Feast. I saw punk rocker and poet Ian Stephens read from *Diary of a Trademark* at Bistro 4, wrapped in caution tape, before he succumbed to AIDS. After witnessing the "stock readings" of the Urban Wanderers Series at Bistro 4, Lee Gotham approached the proprietor about taking over the Monday night slot with a more performative and dynamic series called Enough Said:

> It took two or three weeks to re-establish an audience. The early days were really a fun and surprising success. I just exercised a general criteria of performativity, but not swinging to either extreme of either singer-songwriters and stand-up comedians at the one end of the spectrum, and staid conservative literary offerings at the other. I tried to exclude those two ends but include everything else.

The regularity of the series, every Monday, helped to establish a community based on bohemian ideals, as one participant is quoted as saying in *Impure*: "Aside from being a regular event, it was a social event. And you started seeing the same people perform and the same people going. And to me that constitutes a scene." This community engagement was one of the mandates of the series. As Gotham explains, "there was just as much creativity taking place between the sets, and between people's performances, just in conversations." In 1995, Julie Crysler founded an all-women series at Bistro 4 called Other Muses. This venue helped put the Montreal spoken-word scene on the media's radar. And the community it spawned helped propel the next series at Bistro 4 into existence, foregrounded by force-of-nature Jake Brown and poster artist Billy Mavreas.

YAWP! was the brainchild of Jake Brown, an out-of-work English prof with dramatic inclinations. It was as if Brown was the embodiment of Whitman's barbaric yawp as he performed his "quasi-academic shaggy dog stories" on stage, sometimes naked or covered in paint. You never knew what would happen next. He took over the Monday night slot from Enough Said and his first show was August, 1995: "I was addicted instantly, because to me, it was like everything that thrilled me about teaching a university class, except wild." These events were very popular, and audiences spilled onto the street (in this case, The Main). Brown gave Rufus Wainwright a frequent forum, beyond his regular gigs at tiny Café Sarajevo. YAWP! eventually outgrew Bistro 4 and moved into larger theatres where it brought in bigger acts, both musicians such as Ray Manzarek from The Doors and performance poets like bill bissett.

Mavreas credits his involvement designing posters for the venue as a turning point in his artistic career. "The only thing I was doing for a long time was YAWP! posters. And that's how I was recognized in the comics community." The posters for these shows also caught my attention and meeting their creator was one of the catalysts to begin Conundrum Press with *Mutations: The Posters of Billy Mavreas* (1997) for which Jake Brown wrote an introduction. Many of the performers at the venue had their first writings published in *Fish Piss*, including Heather O'Neill, Jonathan Goldstein, Golda Fried, and Catherine Kidd. In fact, it was the curation by Brown through YAWP! that seized on the formula of featuring different genres like music, comics, and literature in one place that became emblematic of the Montreal scene and so closely paralleled the editorial mandate of *Fish Piss*.

Le Cheval Blanc, a micro-brewery on Ontario Street East in the heart of the downtown Centre-Sud, was another important venue. One of the reasons was that bartender Simon Bossé was also a cartoonist and publisher of the zine *Mille Putois*. He brought in many francophone comic launches and treated the walls as a gallery for the same artists. In essence, Bossé curated the venue, bringing francophone and anglophone comic artists together for events, many of whom Bossé silkscreened onto the covers of *Fish Piss*, notably Siris, Hélène Brosseau, Caro Caron, and Henriette Valium. However, the venue also featured a bilingual spoken-word series called La Vache Enragée, hosted by Mitsiko Miller. The way Miller describes these events is another perfect example of the contact zone that is Montreal culture: "I think the first initial impulse was to make each, anglophones and francophones, discover different forms of literature that were more oriented towards *oralité*. It was really a selfish image of my taste, and I wanted to share it with other people. It's just that it ended up having a political aspect by bridging the gaps between the two communities." Given the cross-pollination of the venue, it is no surprise that Le Cheval Blanc hosted a launch for *Fish Piss* #5 on January 6, 1999. The poster by Siris billed the event as "local magazine madness verité."

Mauro Pezzente and his partner Kiva Stimac first moved into a large space on Van Horne in 1995. However, after less than a year, exhaust fumes and odours from the mechanic's garage directly below forced them to vacate the building. Shortly thereafter, the lease was taken over by Efrim Menuck, who took the first three letters of the area's postal code, H2T, and used the NATO phonetic alphabet to create the space's new name: Hotel2Tango. Godspeed You! Black Emperor recorded the bulk of their first album, *f#A#∞* in the loft's large main room, and it was released in August, 1997. As Lucinda Catchlove writes in her retrospective of the band: "It's easy to mythologize the early days of Hotel2Tango, but its influence on Montreal's musical development and aesthetic is undeniable." The venue provided a nodal point for a new generation of musicians who gathered and experimented, formed their own labels, and eventually outgrew the space. In 2000, Stimac and Pezzente opened the bar/café/club Casa del Popolo on St-Laurent and founded the Suoni Per Il Popolo festival, "continuing the early Hotel2Tango tradition of making space for odd music, arts and crafts, and community." Stimac explains, "Mauro was a touring musician at that point, so he knew what it was like to play a venue. Even though it was very DIY—just a stage and a storefront, we tried to have good sound and lights, and respected musicians." When the Casa proved too small, they rented out the Spanish Social Club across the street. The Sala Rossa became a hub of the local scene, but continued to serve Montreal's Spanish population. "I have a vested interest in this community too, not just the community that comes and goes," states Stimac concerning their ethos. "Like how we work with the Spanish community across the street. It's very important to me. It's not just that we took over this building and made a hip venue." Casa hosted comics launches, performance art, spoken word, and post-rock mixed with avant-punk and jazz. Often the waitress serving you your drink would be on stage the next night. "I have a certain amount of pride," says Stimac, "that people always tell us that, even though we're anglophones running this place, there is really a crossover through these weird music communities of the francophones and anglophones." It is this crossover culture between languages and artistic disciplines through nodal points like Casa del Popolo that made Montreal such a rich a contact zone and breeding ground for bohemia.

Fish Piss represented Montreal bohemia. Crossovers between "scenes" and an open submission policy made

Louis the ideal editor. "I just think of myself as being somewhere between a lot of scenes," he says.

> I say between, but I don't even mean that there are rigid lines between those scenes as such. Like Billy Mavreas being very much a part of the YAWP thing. But he's also very respected in the comics scene. Aside from comics, there's Howard Chackowicz who did the cover of *Fish Piss* #3, who has done some work on Golda Fried's chapbooks and Jonathan Goldstein's chapbooks. That blurs the line again. He's also in a couple of bands [American Devices, Nutsak], so the music scene gets mixed in there. I think the most special thing is that we're all walking distance from each other and our bars, restaurants, and [the] little places that some of us are starting. I'm noticing it has an effect.

This fluidity between genres and languages made *Fish Piss* unique as a zine, but also unique as emblematic of a bohemian community. There was no specialization as other fanzines would have. The crosspollination *was* the specialty, and meant writers, musicians, and comic artists were all equal on the page and in the neighbourhood where they were all "walking distance" from each other. So as a bohemian community, it was not just the writers, or just the musicians, that were making the "scene." It was all of it combined in one location. In the history of bohemia this is similar to the Greenwich Village of the 1960s with Dylan playing the coffee houses, the Velvet Underground and Warhol's Factory, Ginsberg and the Beats still hanging around, and the *East Village Other* publishing underground cartoonists. But the difference is language. In New York the artists were working in the culturally hegemonic language; in Montreal there was no hegemony. In this sense, Montreal at the time was a combination of Greenwich Village and the Latin Quarter of Paris.

But as the metaphorical definition in issue #5 states, fish piss is "Something you're involved with without noticing it," so too were we in Montreal involved in various cultural fields without really knowing what was happening outside of them, isolated due to language but also because no one was paying attention. Unlike Yorkville in Toronto or Haight-Ashbury in San Francisco, there were no bohemian tourists. No one from the middle class came on a bus to check out the freaks. When we managed to make the cover of an alt-weekly, a few locals might take notice but the coverage outside that was zero. Until of course, the music scene exploded internationally and *Utne Reader* placed the Plateau on their global top five neighbourhood list.

In one review of Rastelli's 2007 memoir of those times, the comparison to previous bohemias is made explicit:

> [Rastelli] has successfully painted a timeless portrait of the spirit of bohemia that not only permeates the vibrant and colourful Montreal neighbourhood in

> which he lives and loves, but would feel equally at home in Greenwich Village, Soho or along the left bank of Paris. And, like the Plateau itself, *A Fine Ending* shines with both substance and style.

Or in this *Broken Pencil* zine-of-the-month review of #2: "Fascinating reading—no—essential reading for anybody interested in the Canadian underground… *Fish Piss* tears the roof off your skull. It's like the Renaissance of depravity, the Enlightenment of perversity! Dare I say it—the best minds, the most-addled bodies of our generation all in one fucking zine for two lousy dollars!" Notice the reference to the defining text of the Beat Generation, Ginsberg's "Howl." This review is an early indication of the role of *Fish Piss* as a seminal text for a new bohemia.

Literature

I WAS LIVING IN a huge apartment on Fairmount in Mile End. I was paying next to nothing in rent and shared the space with a number of roommates, one of whom was Catherine Kidd. She used to walk around the apartment talking into a handheld tape recorder. Soon I saw her perform what she had been mumbling. She wore a bloodied butcher's apron and blew everyone away with her talent. I realized that this was what was being called "spoken-word". I approached her to make a book out of her performances, and she went to work making a cassette with DJ Jack Beetz. In 1996, we launched *everything I know about love I learned from taxidermy* at one of those illegal lofts rented out by the writer Ibi Kaslik (who would go on to publish *Skinny* and *The Angel Riots*). Rufus's sister Martha Wainwright played her own songs for the first time, and Corey Frost, a fellow spoken-word artist, flew in from Japan to perform as well.

I was so naïve at first that I did not consider standard paper sizes and consequently had to cut every single page of *taxidermy* by hand. So when the book kept selling, and I had to make more, I figured out to adjust the size. But it was still labour intensive. On one of those early print runs (on the photocopier of course), I used the offcuts and made a book of one of my own short stories. Remarkably, writers with whom I had been associating were happy to have me make their stories into little books. Conundrum Press was born! It must be understood that there was very little support for anglophone writers in Montreal other than doing it ourselves. If you wanted to be published, you moved to Toronto. Period. There was a huge gap between the talent and the infrastructure to support that talent. I quickly realized that through Conundrum Press, I could attempt to fill that gap.

A couple of years later, Billy Mavreas had moved into that apartment and we split the four bedrooms between us, giving us each an "office" or "studio" space for the first time in our lives. The apartment had gunmetal grey plywood flooring, and we painted every room a different outlandish colour. The living room was bright blue with lime green trim. A Saturday morning cartoon apartment. Billy went around adding "spells" to the door jambs, or at the back of closets. Every few days, I would stumble on a new one, a tiny cursive surprise. In the total of eight years I lived in that apartment, we were robbed three times. Each time CDs, knapsacks, and computers were taken. Across the alley was a pawn shop and a strip club. I regularly visited the pawn shop searching for my blueberry iMac. They acted coy. The fridge was so old, ice would build up like a glacier. Trying to thaw it, once, I punctured the tubing containing the noxious refrigerant. There was an old couch on the back balcony. It contained a beehive, so guests would be warned to sit down slowly and carry an EpiPen. It was from that couch, with a view directly into the neighbour's apartment, that we witnessed the true definition of *balconville*. Billy had recently quit his job in shipping and receiving at HMV and had taken over one of the rooms to paint. He created giant canvasses with a simple alien icon on each one and called the series *This is Science Fiction*.

Around this time, smoking was banned in Montreal bars. The city was the final holdout in the country, and I had no idea how some of my friends were going to cope. Overnight, all the cigarette vending machines in the city became useless and were headed for the dump. Inspired by an art project in the US, Rastelli bought one and converted it to sell mini books. Louis called it Distroboto. I quickly realized cigarette vending machines had the potential to be an alternative distribution network, and I knew I wanted to be involved.

Billy's friend Valerie Joy Kalynchuk had been evicted from her apartment and was sleeping on our (safer) red velvet indoor couch for months at a time. She was making zines with Billy and publishing short stories about her childhood in Winnipeg in *Fish Piss*, which I thought were really intense and funny. Valerie's stories which appeared in *Fish Piss* #5 (1999) were "Got the Devil in My Pants" and "Recess Treat": "There is a rumour around school that I am not a girl. This lasts for about five days until Shayna starts telling everyone that Tammy's dad is having an affair with the grade three teacher. No one questions my gender anymore, and I breathe out a sigh of relief and thank God. But I do not stand up for Tammy." Her stories in *Fish Piss* #6 (2000) were "Mineshaft" and "Drinking from the Gravy Boat."

I realized I could make a book of these shorts for the launch of the Distroboto machine. We took the stories she published in *Fish Piss* and made the tiny book *All Day Breakfast*. I asked friends who smoked (which was almost everyone at the time) to give me their empty cigarette packs. One writer showed up with a garbage bag of them, disgusted with herself. I spray-painted the packs silver in my furnace room and added a sticker with the title. I ran across the street to the cheap breakfast joint La Plus Belle Province on Parc and asked to borrow a menu. They were very confused, and thought I wanted take-out. "No, I want to take a menu and copy the picture." After they had reluctantly agreed, I ran home, scanned the day-glow breakfast, ham, and eggs for only $2.50, and ran back to return it. I used the silver-foil paper from the cigarette packs as endpapers. The book fit nicely into the cigarette packs, and I made fifty copies for the launch. Valerie was very happy.

I remember that first machine and walking the five blocks to Rastelli's place to help move it the night before the launch. It was brown and weighed at least three hundred pounds. Rastelli's apartment appeared to be in a state of being half-finished. There were board games in the kitchen cupboards, *New York Times* piled everywhere, filing cabinets, and the walls in the dark living room were unfinished drywall.

We drooled over his industrial stapler which had a metal section to rest the open book, like a pitched roof, before the arm came down hard on the crease with the staple. We had a hand cart, but it still took five of us to get the Distroboto vending machine the one block to the newly established Casa del Popolo. Thankfully, Rastelli lived on the ground floor. *All Day Breakfast* sold out at the launch.

Conundrum needed four books to apply for arts funding, so I expanded *All Day Breakfast* into a small pocketbook. Valerie was excited to write more stories to reach the book's minimum page quota as required by the funder. The newer stories were short, dark, disjointed non-sequiturs, and filled with the trauma of her upbringing. I put her pills on the scanner and used the resulting image as the cover and worried I'd be sued by Big Pharma. I had published a book of Billy's psychedelic posters, printed at a sketchy print shop that was owned by one of his myriad Greek "uncles" who shouted at me, "Cash only!" But that had been stapled and not perfect bound, so we put together a book of his comics with the help of Crunchy Comics, *The Overlords of Glee*, about uncaring god-like bunnies who tease humans mercilessly. Lance Blomgren had written a series of vignettes about Montreal apartments, including mine, called *Walkups*. It was like an updated *Balconville*, but filled with spleen. We made up the advance praise ourselves. And of course, there was Kidd's book and cassette. (She also had a story in *Fish Piss* #4 called "virtual flight into terrain" and in #5 "you are a tea bag, my love.") It would be many more years before I could pay myself a dime, but Conundrum was up and running.

A fifth title, the most ambitious, was an encyclopedic account of the Montreal spoken-word community by frequent *Fish Piss* contributor Vincent Tinguely and Victoria Stanton, who made a monthly zine called *Perfect Waste of Time*. More relevant to the project was the fact they were part of the poetry performance group Fluffy Pagan Echoes, so they were definitely qualified to make such a book. The same could not be said of me. For *Impure: Reinventing the Word* (2001), they interviewed seventy artists, English and French. Publishing it was definitely biting off more than I could chew, with the French and English text translated by Susanne de Lotbinière-Harwood and formatted side by side. The oral history was a perfect example of the contact zone unique to the publishing field in Montreal. The events and performances themselves embraced crossover between languages. For example, Le Groupe de poésie moderne was the francophone equivalent of the Fluffies but often performed on the same bill. In the book, it is discovered that some francophone writers perceived the anglophones as coming out of the American Beat tradition, and New Yorker John Giorno was interviewed, who had performed with William S. Burroughs. Many of the *Fish Piss* contributors were interviewed for *Impure*, including Rastelli and myself, Catherine Kidd, Golda Fried, Jonathan Goldstein, and Heather O'Neill.

My introduction to the entire Montreal literary "scene" was when I was approached by Corey Frost to write a review of the Enough Said series for the spoken-word zine he had wrestled from the Federation of English-language Writers of Quebec called *index*. My review was in a Hunter S. Thompson style, and it was called "Fear and Loathing at Bistro 4," and it was absurd, but I thought it caught the community of chaos that was happening around me. The first few issues polarized the Montreal writing community (partly because members of the Federation were rejected from the zine) and really solidified a new generation who were less based in the academy and more about the street-level, grassroots movement taking hold. Articles in the mainstream press took notice but were baffled. In his listing of all the Anglo-Quebec periodicals from 1976-2006, Concordia professor Jason Camlot writes of *index*: "In its second phase, it was self-consciously irreverent, and even antithetical to what its earlier manifestation stood for."

After Frost took off to Japan, and I had started Conundrum, I became more involved in *index*. The zine came out monthly, so we met every week just to figure out the next issue, since we were essentially making it up as we went along, including design, advertising, printing, and distribution. Around the same time, I was approached by an older gentleman named Graham McKeen who had written his autobiography and needed an editor. He had been friends with Jack Kerouac in the 1950s and had drunk with him in dive bars and backed him up on the piano for his readings in Greenwich Village. Graham can be seen talking to Leonard Cohen in a Montreal bistro in the 1965 NFB documentary *Ladies and Gentlemen, Mr. Leonard Cohen.* Classic line from Cohen: "Graham, you suffer as much as I do, I like to see that." He had stories of rubbing shoulders with all sorts of famous characters. Norman Mailer had agreed to write the introduction to the book. His obituary in the Montreal *Gazette* called him the "last of the authentic bohemians." As I was working on the edits of his autobiography, frequently meeting Graham in the psych ward or chest hospital, I thought it would be interesting to excerpt a piece in *index*, which we discussed at our next editorial meeting. It was difficult to find something appropriate, but we settled on an incident in 1960 of Graham being stabbed by a jealous girlfriend at a party at the same time Norman Mailer's wife famously stabbed him. Graham showed up drunk at the *index* benefit at IsArt. We had rejected Jonathan Goldstein from *index* for his poem about jerking off, but we happily had him perform at the benefit. As Graham witnessed Goldstein read his poetry, he told me he swore he was watching a reincarnation of Jack Kerouac. In my mind, two bohemias converged.

Jonathan Goldstein was also interviewed in *Impure*, where he recounted his time auditioning for Oralpalooza, a spoken-word stage for the touring Lalapalooza Festival. He had this gem about the magic in the mundane: "Pablo Neruda has this line about those matches that you strike, and they don't light right away. They pause, they hesitate for a second. He describes that instant, it's like a match that forgets it's a match, and then suddenly realizes and bursts into flame… It brings out the poetry in just the little bullshit things that happen."

I reviewed his mini chapbook *a car wash the size of a peach* in *Fish Piss* #5: "Goldstein kneels before the altar of the caesura but does not puke in it. His poems are sparse inflections from a taught heart, not haiku and not trying to be; too Beat to be Basho. There is the Brautiganesque: 'I drink a bottle / of liquid paper / & say / I'm starting over…'" This line makes it into his debut 2001 novel *Lenny Bruce is Dead*. When it came out with the legendary small press Coach House in Toronto, we all thought he'd really made it big. This was Validation with a capital V. This fact was proof that the anglophone writing community had no prospects in the city of Montreal and had to look to the centre of the publishing hegemony in Canada. Jonathan Goldstein published numerous stories in *Fish Piss*. The very first issue features "2 things," issue #2 prints "I am Dick Clark, said Pops," issue #3 "Ramona, or what will Monday be like." The story in #4 entitled "groove" also ended up in *Lenny Bruce is Dead*. One afternoon I saw him on the sidewalk outside my apartment on Fairmount and called for him to stop and wait. I ran to get my copy of his novel for him to sign because I thought it was important to do this. He signed it, *from the Hartley of your pages*. Then it was true. This was proof that Jonathan was the character Hartley from Golda Fried's Conundrum chapbook *Hartley's Stories* (1997). The single-story book for a single dollar is about Golda following around a writer who is trying to come up with a title for his first chapbook, which he wants to get perfect.

Hartley's Stories was reviewed in *Fish Piss* #3 by Vince Tinguely, and it is worth quoting here for its description of how Golda's writing style describes the bohemian milieu:

> *Hartley's Stories* captures the general aimlessness of life in the nineties. Things happen and they don't add up. They accumulate, like jottings in a journal, like details in a dream. Waiting, or not waiting, for a key.

The chapbook is an embarrassing peon to my lack of design experience, although I am proud of the dairy creamers I scanned and used as endpapers. (I seemed to have a thing for scanning breakfast items.) The chapbook with the perfect title Goldstein eventually makes is *Blow Hard Pomes* and is illustrated by his childhood friend, Howard Chackowicz. The two would work together on a number of projects, including a story Goldstein wrote for Howard's first comic for Conundrum (*Howie Action Comix*) about a man and his dog and inappropriate behaviour. Of course, Howard also contributed to *Fish Piss,* including the bloody piñata cover on #3. But the collaborative relationship they formed worked well, proven by winning broadcasting awards for the national CBC radio show *WireTap* (2004 -2015). *WireTap* was very popular and gained many dedicated followers (a weekly listenership of

350,000). The creative bond between writer and cartoonist is indicative of the cultural contact zone of Montreal.

Another reference to Goldstein's first novel comes from cultural critic Ryan Bigge, who stayed in my apartment for a few summers around 2005, occupying my polydactylic cat October while I roamed the wilds of Nova Scotia. Apparently, he got up to his own writing in the apartment, including an essay for *Broken Pencil* #24, "Searching for Breakfast and Bohemia." In it, he quotes *Lenny Bruce is Dead* as an example of the all day breakfast lifestyle: "Everyone runs around trying to find a place where they still serve breakfast because eating breakfast, even if it's five o'clock in the afternoon, is a sign that the day has just begun and good things can still happen. Having lunch is like throwing in the towel."

Bigge writes:

> The complete ten-bucks-or-less culinary tour of Montreal [Including Dustys, Casa del Popolo, and Open Da Night] would require innumerable paragraphs, but already the slackwater appeal is obvious. Artists and dreamers glimpse shabby utopia in a city where time elapsing is signified by another refill of gratis coffee. Hours evaporate, days melt together, leaving behind illustrations, songs and short stories, the creative residue of a city that represents a permanent holiday from expectation. Welcome to the best—and only—Canadian bohemia.

Cover, *Fish Piss* No. 1
Art by Billy Mavreas

SEE PAGE 197 FOR ADDITIONAL *FISH PISS* COVER CREDITS

Cover, *Fish Piss* No. 2
Art by Rick Trembles

Cover, *Fish Piss* No. 3
Art by Howard Chackowicz

Cover, *Fish Piss* No. 4
Art by Jean-Pierre Chansigaud

Cover, *Fish Piss* No. 5
Art by Siris

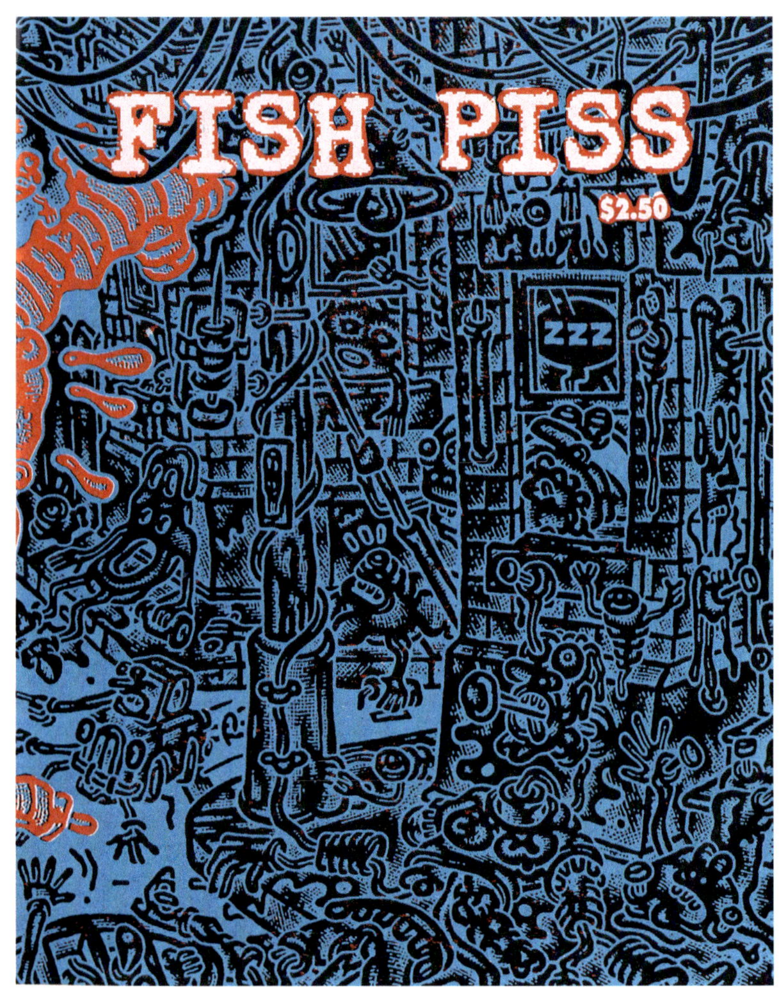

Cover, *Fish Piss* No. 6
Art by Henriette Valium

Cover, *Fish Piss* No. 7
Art by Caro Caron

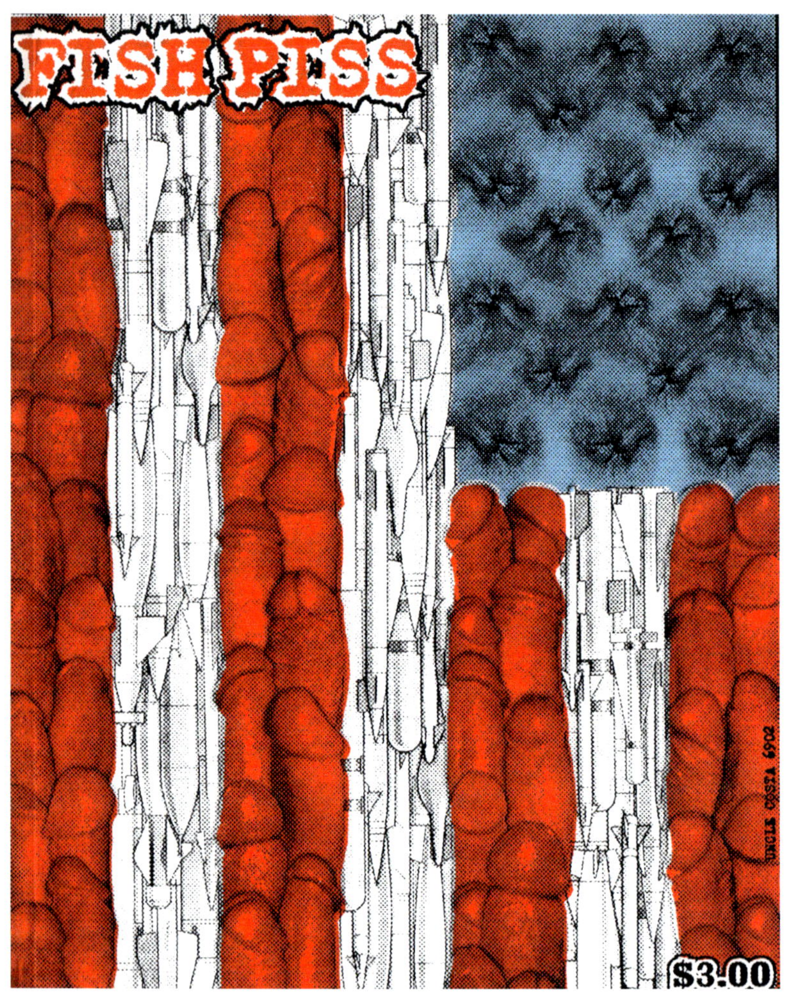

Cover, *Fish Piss* No. 8
Art by Uncle Costa

Cover, *Fish Piss* No. 9
Art by Billy Mavreas

Cover, *Fish Piss* No. 10
Art by Séripop (Chloe Lum, Yannick Desranleau)

Cover, *Fish Piss* No. 11
Tenth anniversary issue — Expozine limited edition
Art by Louis Boutin

Full cover, *Fish Piss* No. 6 (varying colours)
Art by Henriette Valium

Back cover, *Fish Piss* No. 4
Art by Marc Bell

Back cover, *Fish Piss* No. 5
Art by Line Gamache

Back cover, *Fish Piss* No. 8
Art by Dominique Pétrin

Here Bigge is providing a summer tourist perspective of a lifestyle deemed romantic for someone who needs to freelance gigs to pay for an apartment in pricey Toronto. But the point is taken.

Golda Fried published a significant number of stories in *Fish Piss*. Stories of sound checks and girls figuring out how to be women, quoting Bodega songs, complete with cigarettes and goth guys. "glimmer into video" was a story in the very first issue. "everytime I wanted to throw up I had peppermints" and "Ripped out from the Johnny Hassle Entries" were featured in #2. The poem "The locked in clouds" appears in #3. "windows open" appears in #4: "I used to enter his living room like cordless / phones going off." The story "icebox night" is in her first book *darkness then a blown kiss* (Gutter Press, 1998), and it is credited as being reprinted from *Fish Piss*: "We were mostly on the floor. We were digging into the chocolate cake. I was trying to make it last on my tongue. I was trying to fill time and not feel all panicky 'til something substantial happened." Rastelli gives the book a bad review in issue #5: "I get the feeling a lot of the characters and plots are just sketchy because they're practically lifted from diaries and need to be sketchy so no one finds out it's about them." Golda writes a review of hanging outside a Jim Carroll show with her dad in issue #4. Her appearances peter out after that but then the content of the zine also switches to more comics and music coverage—the fiction and poetry disappear.

In 2004, Golda submitted a manuscript called *Nelcott*

is My Darling to Conundrum Press. It was about a virginal McGill student obsessing over a guy who works at a record store. I felt bad rejecting it because I liked Golda, and she was so good-natured. We made a mini book for the Distroboto about her favourite band Royal Trux instead. In the end, *Nelcott* was picked up by Coach House and was ultimately nominated for a Governor General's Award in 2005. That shows me, I guess.

Heather O'Neill had some of her first published work in *Fish Piss*. In an email to me, she explained: "*Fish Piss* wasn't my first publication. But it was definitely a very early one. My first publication was in a kids' magazine when I was in elementary school which I am still super proud of." Her writing appeared over the entire run of *Fish Piss*, from #1-#11, though the poetry and prose tapered off considerably after issue #5. In her 1997 interview from *Impure*, she specifically mentions *Fish Piss* as a source of her work getting into the hands of readers: "Someone I met in Creative Writing at Concordia said, 'We were in a class, and we were discussing your piece from *Fish Piss*.' People are taking it seriously." The piece the class was discussing could have come from issue #1 entitled "2 things," or more likely the untitled piece from #2 (1997) which begins "two eyes are you sleeping? Or do you see what I see" about a young street hustler. Also in 1997, from issue #3, the poem "Do You Want To Be Like Me?" is featured. Issue #11 (limited 10th anniversary issue) reprints a poem of O'Neill's written in 1997, "Love but no Money for the Electricity Bill." Issue #4 prints the poem "home, what." In *Fish Piss* #5 (1999), there is her "excerpt from 'Do Robot Pimps Dream of Electric Whores.'" The "excerpt" in the title implies this could be an early title for *Lullabies for Little Criminals* which she must have been writing at the time as this 2000 interview in *Impure* suggests:

> It seems like everybody's so busy writing books right now, putting together what they've developed in the spoken-word scene in the past few years. Everyone was testing stuff, and now it seems like a lot of people are putting down on the page or recording, or moving on to the next step.

The fact that O'Neill was immersed in the "primordial ooze" of the Montreal community, and benefitted creatively from it, is made explicit in her 2021 introduction to Rick Trembles's book of strips from *Fish Piss*: "I considered that scene where I first encountered Rick Trembles to have been my education as an artist. It was there that I learned to have a voice."

Her first book of poems, *Two eyes are you sleeping* (1998) started as a folded piece of paper with an Edward Gorey drawing on the front and two poems, a very modest zine. The title and some of the poems in the published book come from her work the previous year in *Fish Piss*. She achieved success with her award-winning novel *Lullabies for Little Criminals* in 2006. The book was the winner of CBC's 2007 Canada Reads and was shortlisted for the Governor General's Literary Award for Fiction and the Orange Prize for Fiction, among other accolades.

Other writers living and working in Montreal also shot to Canlit and (world) prominence soon after this period, so there must have been something about the "primordial ooze" in the city which allowed for this. O'Neill is a good example of how the city and its bohemian edge gave space for writers to develop their craft. Yann Martel was living in the neighbourhood and had once come to my apartment for a chapbook launch. One afternoon I bumped into him in the park and asked how the writing was going. "I just submitted my latest book to my agent." That book was *Life of Pi* which would win the Man Booker in 2002 and put our little Montreal literary scene on the global stage.

I was featured on the cover of the alternative weekly *HOUR* with O'Neill and Rawi Hage in November, 2006. O'Neill was just finishing her US tour, I had published a novel called *The Mole Chronicles*, and former taxi driver Rawi Hage was fresh from his huge success right out of the gate with *DeNiro's Game*, which was shortlisted for the 2006 Scotiabank Giller Prize and the 2006 Governor General's Literary Award for Fiction, and won the 2008 International Dublin Literary Award. In a way, these writers were the generation to follow in the footsteps of Leonard Cohen and Mordecai Richler. What they all have in common is a neighbourhood.

As Ian McGillis writes:

> High-profile success stories like Jeffrey Moore [winner of the Commonwealth Prize for Best First Book in 2000], Yann Martel, Madeleine Thien, and Rawi Hage, to say nothing of the force of nature that is Heather O'Neill, plant the idea among the laptop café legions that you can do more than just write here—you can, conceivably, make a living with this stuff.

The writers submitting to those early issues of *Fish Piss* were not thinking about making a living at the time; they were too involved in the excitement of the bohemian milieu to think about projecting themselves onto an "industry." *Fish Piss* provided a safe place to experiment, to work out the kinks and find their voice.

Comics

THE COMICS IN *Fish Piss* probably best exemplify the "contact zone" of the linguistic and cultural field of Montreal. The linguistic otherness of Montreal, and by extension *Fish Piss*, runs parallel to the "otherness" experienced by comics themselves within the cultural field. But we also need to consider the linguistic capital of comics within both the English and French cultural fields. For English readers, these comics would be vulgar, messy, or classified as "underground," and not accessible to mainstream comics readers. *Bandes dessinées* are a highly-respected art form in French, but the BD in *Fish Piss* operate outside mainstream Quebec culture, but also and especially, outside the hegemony of the French linguistic cultural field. There is not a homogenous linguistic market in Montreal, and *Fish Piss* embraces this "heteronormative linguistic field." In fact, both the French and English comics published in *Fish Piss* share more artistic attributes than separate them; they are both outsiders on an underground spectrum. Rastelli explains: "I think the fact that both English and French underground—DIY—independent culture is way off on the margins of the mainstream of either language makes them bond and cross-pollinate more."

As exemplified by Rastelli's unique curatorial process, it is the comic artists who are prioritized in *Fish Piss*. They are the ones getting paid: "The one constant through the run as far as selecting/commissioning was deciding on a cover artist and a centerfold and/or illustrations. The only people who got paid were the cover artist, centrefold artist, and usually one artist per issue providing some commissioned illustrations." The fact that it is the silkscreen covers and comics that give the publication its "otherness" (even within the DIY field) is validated. But who are these comic artists?

The cover of the first issue is a psychedelic fish drawn by Billy Mavreas, perhaps the ultimate crossover artist from the French/English cultures but also the comics/spoken-word communities. "I did the cover for issue #1. It was a time when I was enthralled by that intersection between drawing and writing, so I drew a fish composed of small calligraphic symbols." Mavreas's contributions to *Fish Piss* pre-date his attempts at actual comic stories and are more like illustrated texts, such as "Waiting for the Ride," the centrefold in issue #3, "Hanging with Jesus," and "Tuesday at the Office." This is an artist working out his style in the consecutive pages of a zine. "I think it was the Québécois comix zines in general that are responsible for pushing me into making comics as opposed to graphics or spot illustrations. *Fish Piss* was part of it. It gave me carte blanche which is always good for a young artist."

Mavreas hits the nail on the head. When artists have a forum to work out their style, it influences other artists to work out their styles, and a loop of creativity is formed. "After creating the identity and style of *Fish Piss* in its first issues," says Rastelli, "artists had an easier time coming up with material that fit the magazine, and it made it much easier for me to select stuff. In this sense, artists like Mavreas, Henriette Valium, Richard Suicide, and Marc Bell influenced many younger artists by being part of the first issues which forged the style and identity."

The cover artist of the second issue is Rick Trembles. His autobiographical strips were done specifically for *Fish Piss* and appeared throughout the entire run. Trembles produced a zine called *Sugar Diet* which pre-dated *Fish Piss* and morphed into a forum for his other autobiographical comics. One of the characteristics of his work is its two-dimensional quality, resulting from simple lines with no crosshatching. The characters appear to be constructed of blocks of wood. This allows the writing to be highlighted, and in fact, words often consume the page, his alliterative dialogue filling speech bubbles which become the entire panel itself. But for the comics in *Fish Piss,* he simplifies, strips to the iconic, and privileges the narrative voice. The strips themselves are about seemingly random childhood memories which take on great significance in their retelling. Trembles explains:

> I was roommates with Louis after a midnight move that resulted in my having to temporarily store most of my belongings in my parent's basement. After settling into Louis' I gradually

> started bringing all my childhood belongings back, bit by bit, which started triggering memories from my past. I was worried about them fading from memory, so I took the opportunity to document them before they could vanish. One of my last entries in this series questioned the nature of selective memory, why certain inanities from one's past might resonate more than others, and why, no matter how hard you try, there's no guarantee you can deliberately instigate an event in your life in the present that will pass the test of time as worthy of recollecting years down the line.

A collection of his complete *Fish Piss* strips was published by Conundrum as *Represented Immobilized*, with an introduction by Heather O'Neill, in which she writes, "You cannot speak about the alternative, underground art scene of 1990s Montreal without mentioning Rick Trembles."

Marc Bell was also known for autobiographical strips at the time, appearing in such publications as *Guillotine*, *Mirror*, and later *Vice*. According to Rastelli: "Looking at *Guillotine*, clearly the whole crew of contributors started cranking out the same sort of material for *Fish Piss*." Issue #2 contains Bell's two-pager about an incident when he broke his glasses and walked around "in a fuzzy colourful fog for weeks." Like Trembles, he "instigates the events," highlighting the important decisions that were made while in this state. His relationship fails and he "moves home" only to be beaten up, breaking his glasses again. Here Bell is delving into the traditional nerdy comic artist cliché. Soon after this his career veered away from the autobiographical comics and into the more abstract work of the art world. This is exemplified by his back cover for issue #4. Rastelli gives context: "I used to ask Marc Bell for autobiographical stuff all the time, he did a bunch of that, but then I think it pissed him off and he had his wild phase." It would seem significant that the back cover of issue #4 is Marc Bell's last appearance in the pages of *Fish Piss*.

However, the melding of the art world and autobiographical comics did continue in the pages of *Fish Piss* through the comics of Joe Hale. Rastelli describes his reaction to Hale's work: "His strips looked like some poor kid living in dysfunctional squalor scrawled them out, but they were painstakingly perfected to look like that." These were later collected by Rastelli into a stand-alone zine under the name Spontaneous Productions, in 1999. It is significant that this is the only comics work Rastelli published outside *Fish Piss*. Hale's work was later collected into *Love and Forgiveness* (Swimmer's Group, 2014), edited and with an interview by Marc Bell. Hale appears to be the most significant outlier of the artists published in *Fish Piss*, and he appeared in almost every issue. And whereas most of the cartoonists were happy to have a forum for their comics work, Hale came at the whole medium of comics almost as a performative artistic exercise. Similar to Jack Dylan's lifecycle, Joey Haley created the persona of Joe Hale to explore what he saw as an exciting field of alternative comics, which was specific to Montreal. Disturbing in nature, these works often satirize the autobiographical position taken by many cartoonists of the day, including Bell. Hale's strip in issue #4, featuring a disembodied goose head in a hat, is eerily similar to Bell's greedy goose character. But there was more to it than that: these short stories transcend their small DIY format, reading like classic morality tales gone wrong.

When interviewed, Hale reveals his intentions, like a curtain being pulled back on his artistic practice: "I wanted to satirize the autobiographical format and present a character named Joe Hale who came from a world of unimaginable dysfunction. The formula for the humour in this collection is very dark. The reactions were extreme. For those who loved it, I felt concern for them. For those who hated it, they had my sympathy." It is specifically Montreal where he felt this comics experiment would thrive, possibly due to its value as a contact zone. "I was amazed at how organized the Montreal cartoonists were then. All the high-end stuff was francophone, in my opinion, and I wanted entry. And so, yes, I made Montreal an intentional destination for this pursuit."

Reading his one-page comics in the pages of *Fish Piss*, one did feel disturbed. Comics like "Camp Cancer" or "I Get Wasted" were frank and brutal (*cause I got a pet monkey to beat up, a bag to shit in, and a floor to punch.*). However, reading them today, with the knowledge they were satire, they make more sense, and become a type of gallows humour. But that does not diminish the powerful effect they had at the time, especially on the artists of Fort Thunder in the US, who admit to being influenced by Hale.

The bizarre but hilarious Mr. Graham Falk provides one-page strips, which first appeared in issue #4 and continue in every issue after. His formula is to present a topic in a "how to" format, or like an advice columnist. "Suicide for Cowards," "Everyone Should be Healthy," "Correct Kissing," and "Show Your Pain" (*If you are being overworked then glue a globe of the world to the shoulders of your suit, this will arouse compassion in your co-workers*) are all hilarious in the gag cartoon tradition.

The first graphic novel from Conundrum would turn out to be Marc Ngui's *Enter Avariz* and feature much of the material from *Fish Piss* issues #4-7, including: "Dessert Special with the Boy Ugly," "Zak Meadow featuring Boy Ugly," "Stumped," and "Doghouse," an RIP tribute to Charles Schulz. Then in #9 was the "SARS Exposed" (2003) comic, "an exclusive interview with the latest superbug sensation." Considering I am writing this during another pandemic, it seems nothing changes. When asked about publishing these strips in *Fish Piss*, Ngui responded:

> I loosely kept in touch with Louis through a few friends after I left school. When I heard that he was making *Fish Piss*, I started to submit work. One of Louis' superpowers is the ability to bring

> people together. I don't think I ever received any direct communication from a reader of *Fish Piss* about my work. But clearly it was getting out there with the zine and Louis's efforts to distribute as far as he could.

Of course, the eventual graphic novel is proof that the system worked. Rastelli reviews *Enter Avariz* in *Fish Piss* #9 in which he states: "I always found, from years of knowing many comic artists, that very, very few of them are able to conceive and construct entire worlds of characters in which they can then stage all kinds of adventures. Ngui is one of these artists, and the world he's built up in Zak Meadow is a fertile canvas for some very biting social commentary."

The cover of issue #3 is indicative of the oeuvre of Howard Chackowicz. It features two children at a birthday party, hitting a piñata, but instead of the piñata breaking open to reveal candy, it explodes in a bloody mess of red guts. The two-page strip "The Squirrel Lover" found in issue #2 has the opposite effect on the reader. An old man is broken-hearted when the squirrels run away from him at the park. He then commissions a tailor to make him a suit out of bread. When he returns to the park and lies down, the squirrels surround him and literally eat his love as he cries tears of joy. These two works show the opposing sides of Chackowicz's art, the anguished and the poignant. Also significant is the fact that "The Squirrel Lover" is silent or *sans parole*. The wordless strip straddles the linguistic field, opening interpretation to French, English, or any other language. It is one of the methods to navigate the contact zone of Montreal, removing the language barriers altogether and making the work totally accessible. The silent strip deals in the realm of a shared iconic language. Rastelli hints that this was an intentional choice for *Fish Piss*: "There were quite a few wordless strips in *Fish Piss* which readers did not count as anglo or franco." Many of the *Fish Piss* artists (including Trembles, Siris, and Suicide) contributed to L'Association *Comix 2000* anthology in France which had a mandate to be silent. As Mavreas has said of the anthology: "The book is mute testimony to the potentiality of the medium."

These silent strips were a bridge between linguistic zones, and no one did it better than Éric Braun. Of German heritage but working in the francophone milieu, Braun contributed to every issue of *Fish Piss*. Braun produced one of the better comics anthologies of the nineties Montreal underground, *106U* (pronounced "sans issue"), which featured covers made of metal or fake fur and highlighted Europeans next to the local artists. His *Fish Piss* contributions display a mastery of the iconic language of comics, often with a political message. The three panel gags are populated by characters who could have leapt right off the Monopoly board. As in the game itself, these crooks and money barons deal with a world of simple symbols: a car, a house, a dollar sign, a hat.

Starting with issue #4, the francophone artists begin to dominate the covers and more of the comics content.

The cover of #4 is a street scene by Jean-Pierre Chansigaud who produced illustrations for many issues but no actual comics. Siris provided the front cover of #5 ("Future du Certain!") and Line Gamache the back. The tagline for this issue is: "big variety true false mix o'... whatever." For the first time, the francophone artists outnumbered the anglos. Along with Gamache and Siris are featured: Éric Thériault, Kurt Beaulieu, Éric Braun, Guim, Mr. Swiz, Rose Beef, d. bilos, and Geneviéve Castrée. Siris provides a silent three-page strip called "Traffic Calming" in which his chicken-headed avatar reacts to the urban chaos by smashing all the cars and bulldozing them away.

The cover of #6 is by francophone artist Caro Caron. More women cartoonists (almost all francophone) start contributing to *Fish Piss*, perhaps after seeing other women like Hélène Brosseau represented in the earlier issues, essentially opening a safe space for their work. The fact that Line Gamache edited an all-women anthology at the time called *Une Affaire Gigogne*, which featured many of the same contributors as *Fish Piss*, indicates an understanding of the traditional "boys club" aspect of the comics field and a willingness to try and rectify the situation. A teenage Geneviève Castrée published some of her earliest work in the pages of *Fish Piss*. Dominique Petrin (now exhibiting internationally) provided the back cover for #8. Brosseau appears on the back cover of #9, as well as contributing the logos for various interior columns.

Although never granted a cover or centerfold, the

comics of Richard Suicide couldn't help but shape the "style and identity" of *Fish Piss.* His heavy inking and claustrophobic panels perfectly encapsulate the urban anomie of his downtown neighbourhood in Montreal. His strip in #4, "Oeil de Veau le Cyclopique," is printed with an English translation beside it, the only time this happens in the entire run of the zine. Here Rastelli is testing out the contact zone, perhaps self-conscious that he is introducing anglophone readers to new francophone cartoonists, but he ultimately decides not to continue the practice in future issues. Suicide's strips were later translated by Rupert Bottenberg and collected into the Conundrum title *My Life as a Foot.*

The centerfold of issue #2 is by the cover artist of #6, the legendary Henriette Valium (real name Patrick Henley). Within the context of the Montreal underground comics community, Valium is considered the Pope, and his early contributions brought a real legitimacy to the zine. In fact, his career-spanning retrospective art show at Maison de la culture Janine-Sutto in 2022 was called "*Habuimus papam*—We had a pope." From the gallery catalogue:

> To travel in his universe is to plunge into an infinite and hallucinatory vortex of dark humour and total freedom. This unclassifiable work spans more than four decades of daily obsessive-compulsiveness, existential storms and zones of turbulence. Locked up for long hours alone, he

> finds himself in symbiosis with his art, in permanent experimentation: silkscreens, obscene collages, portraits, micro-editions of his tapes, self-published comics, small films and music together with anxiety-provoking and aggressive paintings to tear out the eyeballs.

Patrick Henley died September 1, 2021. His ashes were appropriately displayed in a silkscreen ink can at his memorial service attended by much of the Montreal comics community. His comics and art have graced almost every anthology and underground publication over the past forty years. Francophone artists revered him, but he was completely unknown in English. As Mavreas says, "The work itself scared and exhilarated us. It's funny and wicked. Lesser talents can play with taboo, but Valium owned it, challenging his readers with their own dark fantasies." Many years after my introduction to Valium's work, Billy informed me Valium had a new book that had taken him seven years to complete, and no one would publish it. Would Conundrum Press be interested? Yes! It was my honour to finally publish his magnum opus *The Palace of Champions* (2016), which won the Doug Wright Award honouring excellence in Canadian comics. When he accepted the award in his ink-spattered rags, he thanked me as "the only one with the balls to publish [him!]" I can't think of a prouder moment in my thirty-year career.

Most of Valium's contributions to *Fish Piss* were pages

from his oversized silkscreened "albums" he'd spend a decade working on. The dense, obsessive rendering of Valium's work helped *Fish Piss* attain another level of underground status, that of a bridge to the European comics field. It should be noted that Valium self-published his albums in both English and French—with two different editions—embracing and helping to define the unique linguistic publishing field of Montreal. So, it is the exposure in *Fish Piss* that allowed Valium to be embraced by anglophones like me, and to bring his work to the North American book "industry" at large.

Which brings us back to the idea that *Fish Piss* acquired symbolic capital over its decade-long run, with Europeans, with anglophones, and with francophones. This symbolic capital created a loop which caused more talented artists to submit. In this sense not only did Montreal shape *Fish Piss,* but *Fish Piss* shaped Montreal (or the Plateau neighbourhood at least). But it also speaks to legacy-building. The zine solidified a serious moment in nineties Montreal culture, what Trembles calls "a time-capsule of various artists' earlier work." With his zine, Rastelli provided a forum for a collection of comic artists to explore, find their voice, and due to the fecundity of the contact zone that is Montreal, thrive.

Music

WITH THE EVENTUAL distribution by Tower Records music became an increasingly important category (via advertising, reviews, interviews) in the pages of *Fish Piss*. When discussing music in Montreal history during the time of *Fish Piss*, one can't help but use the term the "Godspeed Generation." The single most influential band that came out of Montreal at that time, and which led to so many others, was Godspeed You! Black Emperor. The connection to *Fish Piss* is explicit. The band's co-founder Efrim Menuck contributed writing to the zine, and the venue they started became a central bohemian node and even hosted a *Fish Piss* launch.

The neighbourhood also spawned an influential record label, Constellation, and the various artists affiliated with it; the career of Rufus Wainwright, who began as a regular piano player every week at Café Sarajevo; star DJ Kid Koala who opened for the Beastie Boys but also released a graphic novel; and later, rising from the bohemian sink which came before them was Arcade Fire. All these artists broke out of Montreal—some went international, but there were other amazing groups which never busted out but seemed to be everywhere at the time, specifically The Nils; Me, Mom, and Morgentaler; and The Snitches. All of these bands were reviewed in the pages of *Fish Piss*, and some of the members of these groups contributed to the zine.

The origin story for Godspeed You! Black Emperor was recounted in *Wire* in 2000, after the group went international:

> In 1994, Efrim and his friends Mauro and Moya were offered a gig supporting another local group, Steak 72. Rehearsals only began a week before the show.... Don Wilkie and lan Ilavsky had inaugurated their new Constellation label with a 7-inch and a CD by Montreal quartet Sofa... In the meantime, Godspeed had started work on their towering vinyl debut, *f#A#∞ [1995-1997]*, which they originally planned to release themselves as a double 7-inch set. Invited in to help ride the faders during the recording session, Ilavsky and Wilkie offered to put it out as the third Constellation release. By now Montreal's music community was on the upsurge.

I'd heard about the band (one of the drummers was an ex of a treeplanting friend), and the news in the neighbourhood was they had put out an album that was only available on vinyl. Vinyl had not made a resurgence yet. I had released Catherine Kidd's spoken-word on cassette in 1996, but by this time CDs were the thing. But one day in 1997, I checked out a record store on St-Laurent. Sure enough, there was the album. When I bought it, the guy at the counter asked me if I knew what I was buying.

"Sure, they are from the neighbourhood."

"Well, they only made five hundred copies. That's a collector's item."

I took it home and played it on the Fisher-Price record player I'd found at a yard sale for one dollar. Inside the record sleeve was a zine and a crushed penny, presumably crushed on the tracks running behind the studio on Van Horne. I was impressed they included a zine. This was a handmade product, in the tradition of the DIY punk zines, but with classy design and industrial edge. Later I tried to impress my friends by scratching the album on the toy player. They were not impressed.

A reviewer of the album in the influential magazine *Pitchfork* wrote:

> It's hard to articulate today just how alien this record felt back in 1997.... The debut album from Godspeed You! Black Emperor still sounded like nothing of its era, or of this planet for that matter. The packaging for *f#A#∞*'s original vinyl issue—the mournful black-and-white photo pasted to the paper sleeve, the cryptic blueprint-like liner notes and crushed coin contained in a sealed dossier—only seemed to amplify the enigmatic eeriness and

> disorienting dread emanating from the album's string-swept mélange of industrialized drones, field recordings, and desolate twang.

Rastelli had a different take on the album and gave it a bad review in *Fish Piss* #4 because he was comparing the recording to the experience of the performances, often at Hotel2Tango: "Godspeed shows are one of those shows where you can just count on seeing everybody there. You go, drink, hang out, space out to the (preferably) François Miron films, drink, walk around talking to people, smoke, drink, sit and stare like a sheep, snap out of it... Godspeed records aren't quite the same. They're black, totally black, they start with some movie talking kinda like a Pink Floyd record, then it's the same music which is good music. Different, though. I didn't get drunk."

Rastelli launched an early issue of *Fish Piss* at the band's rehearsal space Hotel2Tango. I went to that show to get a copy of the zine and check out the space I'd heard so much about. The venue backed onto the railroad tracks, and all the brick buildings followed the line of the tracks along Van Horne. This was the edge of the known world. Or at least, the edge of the neighbourhood. A sculptor had left large metal artworks on desire lines running through the tall weeds. A water tower on top of an abandoned factory was the block's icon which the band had used on the cover of their album. One got the sense that the entire neighbourhood was abandoned until one heard the whistle of the train. It was as if the streetlights were too shy to turn themselves on. At first, I could not find it. I walked back and forth on Van Horne, late at night, but there was no sign. I double-checked the address on the poster, but there was only a car mechanic at the number. Finally, I saw a slip of paper taped to a door. I went in and up the stairs. Inside were couches and drum kits on Persian rugs. A milk crate, a newly plastered section of drywall—the makings of what I imagined was a studio. Rastelli was selling the zine at the bar. Two dollars a zine. Two dollars a beer. The poet Jason Gallagher—who was frequently published in *Fish Piss*—was on stage, and he was trying to read his poems but everyone was talking, everyone was smoking, everyone was only there for the musicians (the band Exhaust was playing that night), and the poet, who was tall and wore a knit cap, got frustrated and started yelling at the audience, telling everyone in the room to fuck off. And I felt bad for Gallagher, I thought his poems were good, but the contact high was settling in, and I didn't care that much. In the end, Rastelli's review of being at a show in the space is pretty accurate. I was witnessing firsthand how a venue can create a bohemian node.

Efrim contributes "DON'T LOVE MUSIC EVER IT'LL ONLY BREAK YOUR HEART ok?" to *Fish Piss* #9 (2003) as part of the thirty-four-page Recording/Industry Special Feature. It is a stream-of-conscious poetic rendition of his take on the saving grace of music in the shitstorm of the music industry: "I swear there was a time when music belonged to the people, when songs were the things that we made for each other in spite of prettiest wordings or saddest, angriest warblings to pass between us like hugs or handshakes, the sacredest sacrament of peoplehood's dreamings, hopes, resentments & confusions, or like the ringing of chords like perfect bells to smite wicked politicians, judges, or occupying armies ... A SAVING GRACE THAT WAS ONCE AND COULD STILL BE AGAIN..." There are references to Whitman, Joyce, and Shakespeare in the piece which basically tells the tale of the frustration the musician has for the music media when, to him, music is a holy thing. The feature in this issue also contains two stories of K-Tel Records, a personal memoir by Vince Tinguely, his take on the theme *I Believe in Music*, this time coming from the name of the album from 1972, and a history of the Winnipeg-based company by Rastelli.

On May 10, 1998, I went to see Godspeed open for Sonic Youth at Metropolis. By now, I had seen the band at Hotel2Tango. That show had started at the usual Montreal hour of 2am which I found too late. Going downtown to Metropolis to see them as the opening act for a famous, recognized New York band meant they would go on much earlier. But also, I wanted to witness this epic moment of local band makes it big. And that is what happened. I was able to get close because most people were there for Sonic Youth and held back. Godspeed came out with three movie projectors surrounding them on three sides. There were two drum kits and two drummers. They had a light show as well as the films being projected, and someone played the guitar with a screwdriver. It was absolutely amazing. When Sonic Youth came out, they were just a regular pop band in comparison. Godspeed's last concert at Hotel2Tango was November 12, 1998. The experience for the band members changed soon after as guitarist David Bryant asserts: "When we first started out, we pretty much knew everyone in the room. We knew why we were there and why they were there—you could talk to them afterwards, and they told you why. Now we play in front of seven hundred people—they leave, you don't talk to anyone." From there it was touring Europe, Australia, USA, and Japan.

Another legendary venue, and by association bohemian node, from these times was the loft owned by the band The Snitches, which they called C-Pig (Seapig). It closed in June, 2000 and Louis, who claimed to have gone to their shows since 1992, interviewed the hyperactive band member and Word Bookstore employee Scott Moodie in issue #7. The venue's claim to fame was that it was the home of a real pig named Mitsou. Moodie discusses passing the torch to a younger generation who don't know what to do with it, and the already disturbing cycle of gentrification hitting the neighbourhood.

In this article, "Tracing Out an Anglo-Bohemia: Musicmaking and Myth in Montreal," Stahl writes:

> As a social and cultural sphere central to Montreal's bohemian world, the anglo music scene functions

> according to a number of tensions.... We can consider specifically the relationship between language issues, economic and political tensions and their bearing on cultural production and how all can be framed in relation to institutional, industrial, and social networks .... For those who choose to stay, this choice often necessitates the employment of certain heroic narratives, survival myths evincing what Bourdieu has called 'the prestige of romantic triumph.'

Godspeed's co-founder Efrim puts it another way:

> You do feel like an exile living in this city. I feel isolated from whatever the motor of the economy is. I feel completely removed from it, and everyone I know feels completely removed from it. And that's a healthy thing for me.'"

The healthy tension between languages and socio-musical experiences also fueled the next big orchestral group to rise from the bohemian sink of Montreal. As Rastelli says: "Arcade Fire is the same ingredients, but a totally different type of music," about how the Montreal penchant for violins and big bands was evolving in another direction in 2001 when Arcade Fire was formed. "I went to one of their first shows in somebody's apartment upstairs from Barfly, but the first club show was at Casa.

There's the same fertile ground and mindset of openness. A lot of people credit the originality of Arcade Fire to having a couple of linguistic influences."

In the early 1990s, Eric San moved to Montreal to study early childhood education at McGill University and started DJing in clubs. In 1995, when Jon More (co-owner of UK record label Ninja Tune, and half of Coldcut) came to visit Montreal, Eric's innovative and humorous mix tape *Scratchcratchratchatch* ended up playing on the car stereo. Shortly thereafter, Eric, now Kid Koala, became Ninja Tune's first North American signing, and in 1998, he went on the road to open for the Beastie Boys on their "Hello Nasty" world tour. In February of 2000, Ninja Tune released Kid Koala's debut album *Carpal Tunnel Syndrome*. The album received great praise and was featured in the international press for having defied expectation. The album was accompanied by both a video game and thirty-two-page comic illustrated by Kid Koala himself. Eric San contributed to the first and last *Fish Piss*. In #1 was a gag comic. Under the title "The 43rd annual pantomime debate tournament" are two debaters giving each other the finger. Ha ha. His full-length graphic novel, which came out in 2003, was called *Nufonia Must Fall*, and its plotline followed a romance involving a robot. He is the ultimate crossover artist. In fact, he turned the graphic novel into an acclaimed silent film with puppets in 2015. This makes sense based on the interview he gave in *Fish Piss* #10, discussing his childhood: "Well, in my group of friends, half of us were collecting comics; the other half got into records." He discusses DJing sweet-sixteen parties when he was only thirteen, and after moving to Montreal and going to McGill, playing Gert's, "I had to buy records I personally would never listen to," he adds. "But that was the gig that was there, and you learn things like crowd dynamics." He even talks about the feeling he had after making his first album, "All of a sudden I saw the strings and stuff above the puppets." But, it all started with that one mixtape and the DIY distribution on consignment to whomever would take it: "That was in 1996. I was going around in the Plateau, and I would drop off copies in stores that are closed now."

Another *Fish Piss* cartoonist that plays in a band is Rick Trembles, the founder of long-running punk band The American Devices. His two-page comic in issue #10 features his autobiographical rendition of the process of mixing a 45 record in the studio over a couple of months in 1993. Cartoonist Howard Chackowicz plays drums for The American Devices and Nutsak (who were featured at numerous Conundrum events). The late cartoonist and frequent contributor to *Fish Piss* Geneviéve Castrée released an album under the name Woelv with a graphic novel, packaged together, called *Pamplemoussi* in 2004. The book translates the eight songs of the record into images and was reviewed in *Fish Piss* #10 by Rastelli:

> The music is dynamic and building, and is well-served by the backup instruments which, like her

drawings, can be sparse for long stretches and dense for others, all while sustaining an impending mood.

Lhasa de Sela lived an eclectic childhood travelling the States in a converted bus, being homeschooled by anti-materialistic intellectual parents. She went on to live a creative, romantic, and uncompromising life, the life of a "true bohème," before succumbing to breast cancer at age thirty-seven. In her lifetime she became a world-music chanteuse, releasing only three albums: in Spanish, French, and English. Her second album, *The Living Road* was released in 2003 and won a Juno Award, the BBC Radio 3 World Music Award for Best Artist of the Americas, and the *Times* of London named it one of the top ten world music albums of the decade. Its international appeal and multi-lingual aesthetic were natural because the album was a product of the neighbourhood. It was recorded in Masterkut, Jean Massicotte's studio on St-Laurent Boulevard in Mile End. Proof that Mile End's vibe had an influence on Lhasa is in the fact that, on a break between tours, she chose to buy a large stone row house on Avenue de l'Esplanade. She quickly became a regular at the Arts Café on Fairmount where I spotted her numerous times, or swimming at the local YMCA. For the first time in her life she had roots, in "a place [where] she felt so comfortable." For her next album, she wanted to record in English to reach a bigger audience and "as far as finding the musicians to craft a sound, Mile End had what she needed." As Fred Goodman states in *Why*

Lhasa de Sela Matters, "The musicians in this young, anglo neighbourhood were very much in tune with the American alt-rock scene; several local bands, most notably Wolf Parade and Arcade Fire, were on the cusp of US stardom." Undeniably, Lhasa wanted to be a part of the Mile End community which also spawned *Fish Piss*.

Perhaps the most impressive music coverage during *Fish Piss's* run was Rastelli's deep dive into the history of the recording industry over the span of two issues (#9, 10): from 1877 and the publication of sheet music, through to Edison's cylinders in 1913, up to the rise of 78s then 45s and the "battle of the speeds," into the 1950s. To accompany the article, he made a 1901 archival cassette of music. In his introduction, he calls this a "charged topic these days—almost every week there are developments in an emerging new paradigm of records (CD or digital) and the record industry." Note this is before the huge resurgence of vinyl (something Montreal labels were pioneering from the start), and the fear that file-sharing would replace everything and leave the musicians in the cold was rampant. When asked why he wrote such a lengthy history he replied, "to understand what exactly needs to be done to solve the long-standing problems of the record industry, it helps to understand how the record industry got to this sordid point in the first place." The level of research and detail that went into these features is well beyond what a "normal" zine would print. Rastelli hints at his ambitions: "These are a lot of questions for just one magazine article.

What follows is a short, first draft of what will become a series of little books published by the author." However, I could see the twenty-four-page article, complete with bibliography, as the backbone of an academic textbook on the subject.

As the issues progress, music becomes more of the focus of the zine. The first five issues have limited music coverage, then a Music section is included in the remaining issues, with band interviews, a feature on the music industry, and many record reviews. The other big change in the later issues is an increase in advertising, and it is the record labels that dominate. In fact, issue #10 includes the second part of the history of the record industry, an indie record label special section, music interviews, *and* a 45 RPM special section. Of course, there are still lots of comics and alternative news, but the poetry and fiction is an afterthought. It would not seem a coincidence that *Fish Piss* lists Tower Records Worldwide as a distributor starting in issue #5. As Duncombe writes: "The Tower Records chain, under the guidance of zine enthusiasts Doug Biggert and Clint Johns, sold more than five hundred different zines through its bookstores and record outlets," to the tune of over one million dollars in sales. True to the DIY spirit however, the masthead throughout *Fish Piss* thanks a number of individuals in various cities who helped hand-sell the zine to local newsstands. Of course, Rastelli started out as a teenager writing about local bands for *RearGarde* so music is where his heart lies. But it also proves the important link of distribution with content.

An interview by Mike Wooldridge with Tower Records zine-buyer Doug Biggert is reprinted in *Factsheet* 5, #59. In it, he describes his first business trip to Vancouver where he found a zine on a rack and thought, "Why should this mom-and-pop record store be carrying this and not us?" (In case you were wondering if this zine could be *Fish Piss*, the answer is no, this trip pre-dates *FP* by a decade.) Of the titles they carried, Biggert says, "We wouldn't carry them if they didn't sell. But you have to gamble sometimes with zines. I used to argue to my bosses that Tower makes enough money off *Rolling Stone* that we can afford to take a few chances with zines." When asked if there are any rules to publishing zines, Biggert replies: "Generally zines that aren't in it for the money sell better than those that are," and "bright colours are good" on a cover and so is "something that's clever." All these conditions would apply to *Fish Piss*. When asked if making money off of zines is a point of contention, Biggert is forthright: "Some people say the whole distribution business goes against the spirit of making zines." However, he points out, "You can sit in your house in Reno and mail your zine out, or you can go through someone like Tower. You may not make as much money per copy—we're going to have to mark it up so we can make a profit—but you are going to have your stuff read by a hell of a lot more people. You may get letters from Japan or Israel because Tower is over there." This is exactly how it played out for *Fish Piss*. After the distribution deal, letters came in from all over the US, from Ohio, Florida, Chicago, and Baltimore, (at least the ones that were printed).

Fish Piss piggybacked on Tower Records distribution to reach a larger and more music-savvy audience, something that could never happen in today's market, as the former editor of *Punk Planet* makes clear:

> I don't know how you could start a magazine like *Punk Planet* today and do it in print. The distribution just isn't there, and the distribution that is there is fucking evil. The reality is, when *Punk Planet* started thirteen years ago, there were twelve national distributors that dealt specifically and exclusively with the independent and small press—and today there are none.

The reason *Fish Piss* was able to attract the attention of a distributor like Tower Records had everything to do with its symbolic capital. Also, and closely linked, was the fact that *Fish Piss* was being produced in Montreal, a city which was perceived by 1999 as the bohemian capital of music, due to the rise of artists like Godspeed and Kid Koala to name but two, and to some degree the zine provided unfiltered access to this scene.

Politics

In Montreal, so much of cultural production is politicized because of the city's position as a contact zone, both linguistically and economically. An extreme example of how politics permeates the Montreal subculture is the incident in 2012 when Godspeed won the Polaris Music Prize for best album. According to a Montreal *Gazette* article, not only did the band not show up to claim the prize, but "They issued a statement pointing out the contradictions of prizes, galas, and having a car company as a sponsor while the ice caps are melting. Then they donated the $30,000 prize to a program that provides musical instruments to prisoners in Quebec." These are definitely artists used to working outside the traditional capitalist model. Stahl defines this as a specifically bohemian mindset:

> Cultural rebels, "plucky diehards," artists, and café habitues populate a shadow cultural economy, an economy that motivates a world established and cultivated through an underground ideology, one effectively articulated through aesthetic and social codes and embodied in the behaviours, attitudes,

and signifying practices which define a bohemian lifestyle.

As Duncombe has written, "Many zinesters consider what they do an alternative to and strike against commercial culture and consumer capitalism. They write about this openly in their zines." Rastelli is no different. This alternative economy has at least one precedent in the barter system of the zine network as seen in a previous chapter. The reality of the "economic capital" involved in publishing the zine is made explicit in the first issue ($1, no advertising): "I'm about to get this printed five hundred times. The cost is $420. That means this will break even if I sell about 450, leaving 50 for contributors and samples and stuff. After this, it's a full day of folding and stapling, and then walking around to record (and other) stores." It is built on sweat equity. However, while so many were using the welfare system like arts-funding Rastelli worked a day job.

Starting in issue #4 the "For Money" column became a regular feature. Significantly, it appeared every issue until the end of the run. *For money*, meaning what do you do for money, which implies that the creative work you do does not pay the rent. This was the reality of almost everyone involved in *Fish Piss*, but Rastelli expanded the circle so much more. Perhaps appropriately, the first contribution to the column is about begging for change. The next is a story about Rastelli's grandmother who made bombs for the war effort because she was not familiar with needing money in the city since in her town everyone just knew who owed who. Mark Rubinoff writes about his experiences with experimental drug testing in "I, Lab Rat." This was a frequent form of income for people in Montreal who could not speak French. Rubinoff writes a hilarious exposé culminating in his reasons for doing it: "No bullshit here. No ass-kissing, no moving up the corporate ladder, no power games. [They] pay us for our time and our blood. No job stress… All I wanted was my cheque and my freedom… I'd rather be a lab rat than a corporate weasel." Issue #5 features Vince Tinguely's take on being in the army for money. "We were students learning the business of death… What would be abuse in any other situation passes for discipline in the Canadian Armed Forces." Other accounts in this issue are about busking, counterfeiting, and selling weapons. Over the next few issues, Rastelli interviews people about their jobs for the column (now with a beautiful header drawn by Hélène Brosseau): a telemarketer who practices the art of misleading, not lying; another column features someone selling adult novelties. When talking to "C" about scavenging, the economy of the Tam-Tams of the early 1990s is revealed. This was a group of drummers that gathered every Saturday at the Sir George-Étienne Cartier monument in the park below Mont Royal: "People were selling everything at the tam-tams; they were selling food, cooking food even, chips, chocolate bars. They would have cases and cases of beer, but they went too far and attracted the police." Rastelli editorializes:

> Left alone humans can still, with no planning or control whatsoever, get a little economy and society going. After all, no one ever planned the Tam-Tams, which probably started in the 1980s with a handful of drummers and gradually became the underground village of twenty thousand people we all took for granted ten years later.

This comment also describes the anglo-bohemia of the time, an underground village we all took for granted.

Street-level politics was apparent in the interviews with regulars at bars around Montreal, in which they were asked questions about their daily lives. Issue #8 has a lengthy fourteen-page documentary-style history of the corner of Ste-Catherine and St-Laurent, interviewing the regulars of the red-light district, covering the glory days, the decline, the sex workers, hot dogs, and the old LSD guy. This anti-celebrity stance was the norm in fanzines; they provided an alternative to the repressive media saturation of celebrity culture. Rastelli took it to another level, finding interest in the lives of those completely outside society in some cases. As Beaty writes about psychiatrist Wertham's book on fanzines, "He praised the fact that fanzines were not polluted by the greed and arrogance that dominated mass media but instead were something 'intensely personal.' As someone who had become increasingly concerned about the mechanization of daily life as his career wore on, Wertham regarded fanzines as a positive counterforce to the mass media."

Probably the most important political commentary in the pages of *Fish Piss* was in issue #7, the special feature devoted to first-hand accounts of the 2001 Quebec City Summit of the Americas demonstrations and resulting police action. Although the anti-globalization movement can only be loosely defined, a commonality between participants is the opposition of large, multinational corporations having unregulated political power, exercised through trade agreements and deregulated financial markets. In Quebec, thirty-four heads of state met to discuss expanding NAFTA (North American Free Trade Agreement) into the FTAA (Free Trade Area of the Americas). Rastelli explains: "Since the main goal of any such trade deal is the replacement of individual national trade policies with a single hemispheric policy, some or all of the countries involved would lose some control over the ability to govern individually.... This is considered a good thing by multinational corporations, because they consider the cost of dealing with the many different policies of the many different countries to be an unnecessary expense." As soon as word was out that security would be beefed up, no masks would be allowed, a 3.8 km fence or "security perimeter" would separate the delegates from the city, and the local residents living behind the perimeter would be trapped, it encouraged more individuals to go and protest. In Montreal, Concordia University postponed final exams to enable five thousand students to go on rented busses. Students came from other Montreal universities and from Ottawa and the US, though the border security was heightened. And that is just the students. "It would probably be no exaggeration to say that over a hundred thousand people from outside Quebec City arrived to demonstrate."

Rastelli interviews a dozen participants, and the narrative runs chronologically over the next forty-one pages, complete with: tear gas stories ("Nothing signifies the Quebec Summit like massive quantities of tear gas"), arrests, the kidnapping of Montreal anarchist Jaggi Singh as a pre-emptive strike, unhappy residents, marching unions, Sarah Polley documenting the event on film, the stories of injuries from plastic bullets, the Police State in the Making, and coming back home politicized. "When I got back, I was totally rejuvenated. I think the experience did a lot for a lot of people, and I think a lot of good is going to come out of it," confided one participant. A fifty-year old woman and her teenage daughter came from Saskatchewan "and both experienced assaults upon them by their own government and had seen thousands of others inflicted with the same treatment. At the same time, [they] gained more confidence that citizen action can combat corporate control of [their] world." It is a testament to the editorial style of Rastelli that he incorporates so many firsthand, street-level stories in his feature. He acts almost as a documentary director. Rastelli concludes: "Regarding 'anti-globalization' generally, I think that between such large protests everyone should be more active locally. If activists ignore neighbourhood issues because they don't get them worldwide attention, then I'm afraid they've caved in to the worst kind of globalization."

The incident disillusioned and politicized many Montreal artists, and those politics seeped into their art. A perfect example of this is David Widgington and Cumulus Press. Cumulus began in 1998 with a walking guide to Montreal's Old Port, followed by a couple of poetry books. Widgington's energy attracted the attention of Lina Shoumarova, who also interviewed him for her MA thesis on the book-publishing field in Montreal. After his participation in the Summit of the Americas however, his publishing practice was forever changed: "The Summit of the Americas was a key event in my political awakening, and it has influenced my activism ever since. And what is super interesting is that the 2012 student strike—which was the largest protest movement in Quebec—had many people like me, who were politicized in 2001, active in the organizing." After the Quebec Summit, he turned toward publishing more politically engaged books, starting with *Counter Productive*, a document of the Summit in essays, photographs, posters, and audio, similar to the coverage in *Fish Piss*: "After *Counter Productive*, I remember telling myself that I would steer my publishing practice to always have a political angle. I co-founded the video-activist collective Les Lucioles, which lasted five years, I joined CKUT and became a host of an information morning show, and all of this directly related to people I met at the Summit of the Americas." Significantly, on the indicia page of the book is listed *Copyleft 2002: may be reproduced in its entirety, provided it is distributed for free* which obviously subverts the field of publishing entirely but is more common in zines, as Duncombe points out. "Material is expected to be shared and reprinted, or 'borrowed' as zine writers delicately put it." Widgington describes the book on his website: "With still cameras and video cameras, microphones, pads and pencils, we recorded our experiences at the Summit the entire weekend, capturing an intimate and diverse discourse absent in the headlines of most news dailies. We recorded our own history on our own terms." In fact, his publishing practice closely parallels Rastelli's, and it led to finding his tribe among the organizers of Expozine:

> Although I wanted to sell the books I published, I did not want to join the upper echelon of publishers I met at the Association of Canadian Publishers events. They were mostly corporate-minded and I was anti-corporate minded. Obviously, I wanted to succeed in publishing so I latched on to every organization I could, but I never really fit in. Not until Expozine!

Expozine was founded after I wrote an article for the *La Voce del Popolo* zine about how us local culture creators were sick of travelling to Canzine in Toronto when we had so much more to offer in Montreal. "The gauntlet has been thrown down. Who shall pick it up?" Turns out, it was Rastelli and Widgington who joined myself, poster artist Mavreas, and spoken-word guru Ian Ferrier in getting it started. The first

Expozine took place in 2002, appropriately enough at the bohemian node La Sala Rossa, featuring fifty exhibitors of "small press, comics, and zines." In both English and French. The idea was to be inclusive of many different scenes, not just comics, not just books, not just zines (like Canzine) because that was our reality in the contact zone of Montreal. It was also a reaction to the organizers of the Salon du livre de Montréal which wholeheartedly rejected any works in English. In fact, for the first few years we tried to plan Expozine for the same weekend, almost as an anti-Salon.

The other big feature on a political subject was *America Undeterred* in issue #8 (2003), about US foreign policy. The cover is a beautiful silkscreen by Uncle Costa of the American flag with rows of missiles for the white stripes and rows of penises for the red ones. The feature starts with a shocking list of "fronts in the American War" including of course the "Axis of Evil" but so many other countries as well. Rastelli contributes the text equivalent of the cover in "Penis Power: The unsustainable erection of American foreign policy" in which he asks for evolutionary steps toward a better humanity: "In this world, nations claiming to be above the need for global consent, 'super' nations, can only be seen as desperately clinging to past realities, or at worst, desperately committed to destroying the new reality. At the heart of this kind of denial is nothing else but pure testosterone.... I don't believe this would happen if women were in charge." The feature goes on to list the seventeen major international agreements broken by the Bush Administration and ten things you didn't hear George Bush say on 9/11, including #8, "Wow that's some flying!" Also included is Éric Thériault's comic about planning to go to a convention in Washington when the planes hit the twin towers and Rick Trembles's comic strip movie review of *Dr. Strangelove*, with an actual quote from the movie: "You can't fight in here. This is the war room!" Perhaps the most interesting history lesson is about the regime change on a different September 11, in 1973. In it, Rastelli tells the story of Pinochet's coup to take power in Chile and how the phrase "September 11" came to symbolize the lost hope for democracy in South America. Rastelli adapted this article from a small Distroboto book he made for his Time Machine project.

Although other cities are hives for political activity, Montreal was another contact zone at the time, being ruled by a separatist socialist party, in a state of economic decline, with a corrupt police force, and a strident student population. All cultural activity must address the politics of the local landscape because the act of making culture in Montreal, especially in English, is inherently political. *Fish Piss* took a very strong but not extremist stance on political issues: "I've always been firm on the fact that 'doing it yourself' is more of a political act than the content. It doesn't have to be political content. You're already doing something, not so much against the system, but for self-empowerment, if you're doing it yourself." Basically, Rastelli spoke to the people about what the people were speaking about to him. He was a conduit for the middle-class-dropout bohemians to hear the stories of the street. Importantly, he advocated for a new economic paradigm, not just through his words, but through the actions of his sweat equity in making the zine, and making it affordable, and thinking global but acting local, before the phrase was coined.

The Death of Bohemia

WHY HAVE I USED the word "last" for the subtitle of this book? There are a number of reasons, but they all come down to the internet and an increasingly corporate culture that was just ramping up during the run of *Fish Piss.* In fact, when we have Pinterest pages of "boho style," the term bohemian lacks authenticity. Certainly, gentrification killed bohemia, and it has been no different in Montreal, but such has always been the case; bohemia is fluid—it can move. Look at the difference between Montmartre in Paris—essentially a backwater slum in the 1880s—and the expansion of Paris and its subsequent real estate costs. But there were still bohemians in Paris in the 1950s, just in a different neighbourhood. The main difference affecting bohemia today is social media. Social media was not a part of the nineties at all. Facebook started in 2004, Twitter in 2006, Instagram in 2010. Think of Sartre and de Beauvoir in the Café Flore in 1946 and the writers from Saint-Germaine-des-Prés dropping in to discuss their essay in the latest issue of *Les Tempes moderne*, drink more coffee, commiserate over trying to find a cheap restaurant, take notes for a manifesto. Today that meeting would look very different. In an authentic bohemia individuals connect in the shared space of a bar or café; a venue is the nodal point. Today, as the many open laptops would imply, individuals go to the café to connect in the shared space of social media. They go to cafés to *not* connect with the other people in the café, who are also looking at their laptops. Their peer group could be anywhere in the world. The interaction which creates the "ambiance" of bohemia, the primordial ooze, has been lost forever. This is true of the field of zines as well. As the internet became widely available, it provided a new way for fans of various subcultures to connect, and many of the print publications either moved online or simply disappeared.

Mavreas is interviewed in a special edition of the zine *4 Minutes to Midnight* celebrating Expozine's 10th anniversary. Mavreas points out that the scene in Montreal has expanded, so what once was one recognizable scene, whether comics or spoken-word, in the mid-1990s, has splintered into many scenes with minimal overlap, "It's not a Venn diagram." There is so much more cultural activity transmitted more quickly, and the main reason is the internet. "The kids are uploading their entire sketchbook to the internet, willy nilly, and sharing it with people, and then seeing what everyone else is doing and maybe being inspired by that. A zine fair in Montreal, in 2008, looks like a zine fair in Boston in 2008, or in Toronto..." Or like Etsy for that matter.

Some alternative culture from the 1990s went corporate, as the story of the media conglomerate *Vice* makes explicit.

Ryan Bigge has written extensively on *Vice* and how a free underground magazine could make such enormous profits: "*Vice* was founded in Montreal in 1994 by Suroosh Alvi, Gavin McInnes, and Shane Smith. It began as an irregularly published free newsprint monthly called *Voice of Montreal* that borrowed heavily, in both content and style, from contemporary alternative press conventions." It should be noted that co-founder Gavin McInnes, at this time, was authentically invested in the alternative press, putting out his comic zine *Pervert*, including guest artists, some of whom overlapped with *Fish Piss*. In fact, in one editorial, he thanks *Voice of Montreal* for letting him use the computers to print his zine, much like Rastelli at his day job. In an extreme role reversal, McInnes would become a founder of the alt-right group the Proud Boys.

In September of 1996, the magazine was renamed *Vice*. In October of 1998, the magazine abandoned its tabloid newsprint format and switched to a letter-sized magazine format with colour on glossy paper stock. In 1998, when Rastelli was folding and stapling *Fish Piss* #4, hoping to recoup printing costs at two dollars a copy,

> Richard Szalwinski, founder of Behaviour Publishing and Normal Networks… invested between $5 to $6 million in the magazine, *Vice* stores, online retail, and other related brand extensions… by the spring of 2005, the magazine was generating $17.5 million annually…. The co-founders of the

> magazine have been able to elide the contradiction between the underground content of the magazine and the generation of profit.

Bigge references Sarah Thornton's term "subcultural capital" to describe the counterculture credibility *Vice* sought out. This inverted version of cultural capital means that if you listen to the right bands or have a certain haircut you can gain status in the job market, thereby converting subcultural capital into economic capital. Although *Vice* and *Fish Piss* emerged from the same bohemian milieu, with the same "alternative" mission statement, the two publications went in radically different directions. *Fish Piss* remained truly "authentic" and *Vice* skewed its original mandate toward corporate profits under the guise of counterculture credibility. Eventually, even corporate profits were not enough, and in 2023, *Vice* filed for Chapter 11 bankruptcy.

Gregory Pierrot in his book *Decolonize Hipsters*, spills quite a bit of ink on *Vice*, what he refers to as "a lad magazine for the Williamsburg set." He makes the explicit connection between *Vice* and the origins of hip, that of the appropriation of Black culture, and explains how problematic that relationship became, eventually culminating in one of its founders forming a racist sect: "*Vice* rose from punk fanzine to multimedia empire along with the newfangled hipster scene it both sprouted from and helped go global. *Vice* became known for approaching topics, serious or outlandish, with a trademark tongue-in-cheek tone, an in-your-face aesthetic and hefty servings of misogyny, homophobia, and racism—a spirit echoing that of bourgeois-shocking avant-gardes and provocateurs for a century or two." He also examines the hipster as a cliché invested in corporate culture. "Like all clichés the hipster has become part of the décor, a nuisance from the past woven so seamlessly into the fabric of our days that we no longer notice. There's no telling the hipster from the douchebag these days…" Pierrot is also horrified to see Kim Gordon of Sonic Youth on ads for The Gap. As he states, "I hated that I had been made to look at commodities I had no interest in, simply because of the clever use of people I appreciated for their music."

When video-game juggernaut Ubisoft moved into the old brick Peck Building at St-Laurent and St-Viateur in 1997, it slowly changed the landscape of the neighbourhood. Many new hip lunch places opened on St-Viateur. The scruffy artists populating the streets were replaced by geeky twenty-somethings with oversized headphones. Starting with fifty employees and growing to thirty-five hundred—most of whom were hired after 2002—they brought money to the neighbourhood. Soon, designer furniture outlets proliferated instead of funky cheap studio lofts. Although one of the largest game development studios in the world, it participates actively in the neighbourhood, including reviving the St-Viateur St-Jean-Baptiste street festival (previously closed due to riots), and providing work to some artists (Catherine Kidd won an Actra award in 2019 for her voice work on the game *For Honor*). But one can't argue with gentrification.

The steady corporate co-opting of bohemia in advertising has thinned the primordial ooze until it is indistinguishable from tap water. An example is Apple's "Think Different" ads that ran from 1997-2002 that used images of Ginsberg and Kerouac, and in fact used Kerouac's lines from *On The Road,* "Here's to the crazy ones" for a commercial. This is nothing new. In *Making the Scene*, Stuart Henderson writes of the dissolution of the hippies of Yorkville: "By appropriating hipness and taking up a position behind its wheel, steering it around the corners, advertisers helped both entrench the binary understanding of hip versus square and to demolish the sense of authenticity that any of the first waves of Villagers had cherished about their community."

Of course, today the word "bohemian" has taken on a different meaning than it has historically. In fact, "authentic bohemian" is now an oxymoron. Specialized marketing campaigns have made a bohemian into someone with a certain style, someone who caters to a fashion, in other words *in*authentic. However, the term "authentic" itself is heavily ambiguous. What is authentic? And through whose POV? Sartre simply put the complexity in 1947 with the line: "If you seek authenticity for authenticity's sake, you are no longer authentic." Duncombe reminds us what passes for authentic in the zine world. "Saying whatever's on your mind, unbeholden to corporate sponsors, puritan censors, or professional standards of argument and design, being yourself and expressing your real thoughts and real feelings—these are what zinesters consider authentic."

When I was doing research for this book, I came across the listing for a book called *Bohemian Manifesto* by Lauren Stover. You can imagine my excitement at finally having access to the answer, finally knowing definitively, what is a bohemian? However, when the book showed up, I was quickly disillusioned. Turns out Stover is known for her previous book *The Bombshell Manual of Style*, and she treats bohemianism very much as a style. She examines bohemian food and clothing and bohemian stationary, and astrology. She breaks bohemians into different categories: The Nouveau Bohemian (has money), The Gypsy Bohemian (folksy flower child), The Beat Bohemian (reckless, raggedy, utopia-seeking), The Zen Bohemian (meditative but in a rock band), and The Dandy Bohemian (polished, even when wearing tattered clothes). Obviously, she is considering modern bohemians as inauthentic. To her credit, she attempts to define the bohemian, but she does it from a point of fashion, of style, not substance. In fact, she even asks, "Can and do Bohemians exist today? Can you own a DVD player and a BlackBerry and be a bohemian? Yes and no. It doesn't matter." She admits we will never be able to recreate the conditions of the Left Bank bohemians, or even the slackers of Gen X, but what we can do is "embrace our creativity" which is a pretty watered-down "manifesto," if you ask me.

Henderson acknowledges this authenticity in reference to the "real hippies" of Yorkville: "This notion of 'real hippie' or the 'true Villager' had begun to matter a great deal… This authenticity—loosely defined, impossible to quantify—seems at the very least tied to commitment." He recounts a very interesting incident which shows the complexity in the term. After the Yorkville scene had been discovered as a place to "drop out" and catch the wave of bohemia, the CBC's Knowlton Nash took to the streets to do a documentary on what was happening. He interviewed a young man who was supposedly a real hippie: "If enough people drop out of society, it will be altered," said the young man on camera. "It may eventually be the creation of a subculture. A large enough subculture could modify the existing culture." What was revealed many years later, however, is that the young man being interviewed was paid $500 (an enormous sum when lunch cost less than one dollar) to read from a script. So, it would appear the young man, not to mention Nash, was inauthentic. But let's dig deeper. Turns out the young man was William Gibson, who would go on to become a very famous science-fiction writer. And it turns out he wanted to get out of Yorkville to escape the inauthentic hippies that had moved in (if the CBC had discovered it, it must be already over), and $500 could get him pretty far. He "performed" for the camera to facilitate his escape from inauthenticity. The fact that he became a dedicated writer would imply that he was *committed* to a life of cultural production, therefore *authentic*. So, coming full circle he is a "real hippie" after all.

In Montreal, during the time that *Fish Piss* was being published, there was no ambiguity over authenticity, mostly due to language. Everything in the anglo-underground arts community by necessity had to be authentic; no one from the CBC was coming to document us. The CBC was only interested in French culture. If no one is watching, there is no need to put on a style for the camera. So, we did what we felt would further the community, we were committed to creating our own culture, committed to advancing our craft, whether writing, drawing, music, or art. Today, the anglophone culture creators that weathered the storm have moved into cheaper neighbourhoods, and importantly, placed their children in French schools for the most part. This means they are investing in the bilingualism of the city, and in fact, now participate in the mainstream hegemony of francophone culture, leaving a purely anglophone bohemia behind.

Another reason bohemia fails is because it is difficult. Poverty is stressful. One needs money to live, so rising rents are a problem, but one also needs to be able to fuel the creative impulses that cause bohemia in the first place, or they disappear. Authentic work, or sweat equity, as I have called it, takes its toll both mentally and physically and is ultimately not sustainable. In an editorial written after the Ice Storm, Rastelli explains what a toll it takes on him to juggle the two sides of his existence:

> It's been a long, hard task making this *Fish Piss*. I've had to be in an office building every day of the week to make the money to pay for it. The rest of

> the time, I've tried to balance between living the way life is well-lived in this city, and pissing out, releasing what it is about life here that's important to write down.

This is the same reason the editors of *Factsheet Five* have claimed for its demise. Working very long hours for little or no money.

Can there ever be another authentic bohemia? Not as it was originally defined, no, because the definition of bohemia has radically changed. As Duncombe writes:

> No longer is there a staid bourgeoisie to confront with avant-garde art or a square America to shock with counterculture values; instead, there is a sophisticated marketing machine which gobbles up anything novel and recreates it as a product for a niche market.... The underground is discovered and cannibalized almost before it exists.

He claims a *geographical* Bohemia (like Paris, or Williamsburg) is dead but holds out hope for zines, which are created in the suburbs and small towns, creating a new *bohemian diaspora*: "With coffeehouses owned by corporations and traditional bohemian neighbourhoods populated by middle-class professionals, zines offer an invaluable service, acting as café, community centre, and clubhouse that help connect these bohemians to one another, providing the cement that holds together a dispersed scene." He credits the term "bohemian diaspora" to C. Carr, "for the first time in 150 years, bohemia can't be pinpointed on a map." Priced out of traditional bohemias, new bohemians moved elsewhere and were soon followed by professionals who wanted the thrill of living in a bohemian-style community. The cycle of gentrification continued, with artists playing the role of "shock troops." This cycle has been a familiar one for many decades, as far back as 1926 when Floyd Dell was lamenting the fall of Greenwich Village: "These little restaurants served to advertise the Village to the people from uptown, who presently began to come on sightseeing tours, with their pockets full of money and their hearts full of pathetic eagerness to participate in the celebrated joys of bohemian life." Eventually these new bohemians scattered across the country and de-centralized. Having a few blocks in an urban centre where one hundred or so artists and their families live is vastly different than the same families scattered across the university towns and suburbs. I tend to disagree with the idea of a bohemian diaspora. Remember Duncombe was writing in 1997, certainly a peak time for zines, but social media did not exist yet. By definition, a bohemia implies gathering in person, hence the importance of venues. As the title of Henderson's book makes clear, making the scene "suggests that the hip folks recognized the power of presence in creating meaning in any particular locus." A zine is not a venue, nor is it an objective space to gather subjective ideals. It is personal and subjective.

Communicating through the letter pages of zines certainly is an alternative network, but not a bohemia. *Fish Piss* did not create a bohemia by networking with creators of other zines in other cities; it brought together contributors of many stripes who themselves were gathering in venues in a geographic location of Montreal, and it was the nodal point of the zine—the Venn Diagram—that facilitated the bohemia.

When cities are ranked according to their Bohemian Index, you know "bohemian" has lost its meaning. This is a term Richard Florida defined in his bestselling 2002 book *The Rise of the Creative Class.* Bohemians, who used to rebel against the values of the middle class, are now card-carrying members of the Creative Class (30% of US workers), whether they know it or not. In his book, Florida argues that "places with high concentrations of gays and bohemians tend to have higher rates of innovation and economic growth," where "offbeat ideas are not stifled but are turned into new projects." In essence, being a bohemian gives you a competitive advantage in the marketplace. This is completely the opposite of an authentic bohemian, who is trying to navigate an alternative to traditional capitalism without starving. One of the ways Florida empirically measures and ranks cities is through a Bohemian Index. This is defined as "a measure of the density of artists, writers and performers in a region." His conclusions are that "rather than being driven exclusively by companies, economic growth was occurring in places that were tolerant, diverse and open to creativity—because these were places where creative people of all types wanted to live." Ubisoft, the largest video game company in the world, chose to settle in Montreal at the time of a recession, after all. Creativity has become its own industry, and Florida argues that the creative industry and its economic influence is surpassing other industries, to the point where a new class must be defined. Florida further elucidates his argument in commenting on the tension between the age-old Protestant work ethic and the "hedonistic" bohemian ethic:

> Many observers have noted the clashing of these two value systems, and recently some have commented on their blending—usually with the conclusion that one or the other has been watered down, or spoiled in the process.

But Florida claims this is using old models and suggests something new: "the shared work and lifestyle ethic that I call the creative ethos." Here we have bohemianism twice removed. Basically, Florida, in this highly influential book on socioeconomic systems, dismisses bohemianism by turning it into a measure of a neighbourhood's desirability to access employment, which undermines the initial meaning of the term. As Ryan Bigge points out, Montreal ranked fourth on Florida's Canadian Bohemian Index, behind Victoria, Toronto, and Vancouver, which means we can't take it too seriously. Bigge's article implies

Montreal should be ranked first. But Florida's ranking here is also proof that the scene in Montreal was flying under the radar at the time. Bigge suggests a "Breakfast Index" would be more accurate.

And what about this idea that bohemia can only be recognized in hindsight, as one Greenwich Village guidebook put it. "Whatever else Bohemia may be, it is almost always yesterday." This implies that the people living their lives in the present cannot be bohemians. So what are they in the present? As the editors of *The Atlantic* wrote as far back as 1909:

> The finding of a bohemia for ourselves is conditional on certain alternatives: and here they are. Either we must be very young and very unexacting, or else very old and blessed with a genius for gilding gorgeously our recollections of a tawdry past... Impassioned Recollection is the critic's word... and with that faculty each of us may build him a Bohemia—long after the event.

The idea that bohemia is only impassioned recollection, a mythical place, a spirit, or state of mind is often heard. But if this is true, we can claim it never existed in the first place. This is implied tongue-in-cheek by Marion Magid in her "The Death of Hip" (1965): "Hip does not exist; hip exists everywhere; hip exists only in Warsaw; it is all a semantic problem; it is a socioeconomic problem; it is a fraud, and in any case, not photographable nor possible to interview." If the café or venue defines the bohemian space, then those who frequent the venue on a regular basis, by definition, must be bohemians. With the disappearance of these bohemian spaces, it would be very hard to find anyone today who would call themselves a bohemian, since the term has become a parody of itself. But perhaps this is a good thing. Perhaps finally the authentic worker in the cultural field can be recognized as such and call themselves simply a professional artist. As Robert Dunavon wrote in 1958: "The bohemian served a useful purpose in his day, and, while we may sigh over his passing, we are just as glad his day is over because it means that we are finally on the way to producing that cultural climate in which the bohemian will be unnecessary and the artist will take his place as a useful and respected member of society."

The Legacy of *Fish Piss*

The legacy of *Fish Piss* is tied up in the activities Rastelli has carried over from the nineties, notably ARCMTL, Distroboto, and Expozine, but in a more general sense, it is the legacy that any successful zine, or alternative culture network, provides readers and contributors. To have a safe space to experiment, to work out the kinks, to be one's "authentic self" at least for a time. To make something instead of being fed something. The fact that Rastelli is still going would imply that he has discovered his authentic self, at least partly through the editorship of *Fish Piss*. As Seigel writes, "in the end, bohemia cannot fulfill the promise of utopia for which it alternately served as foretaste and substitute." Or as Duncombe puts it:

> The network of zines embedded within a larger underground culture, creates a forum through which individuals may become able to construct their identity, formulate their ideals of an authentic life, and build a community of support, without having to identify themselves—either positively or negatively—with mainstream society.

Certainly, social media has killed geographic bohemia but what about the argument that the internet has killed all alternative culture? It is no coincidence that Duncombe's afterword to the 2017 edition of *Notes from Underground* is called "Do Zines Still Matter?" In it, he acknowledges that zines are still being published but addresses the rise of the internet. He argues that anyone and everyone can publish on the internet, and as such the cultural norms often conform to "the dominant arbiters of cultural value" which are just an extension of capitalism, "blogs become calling cards for aspiring mainstream writers, Facebook pages become advertisements for one's own celebrity, and so on...."

So yes, zines still matter in the internet age, and by extension the legacy of *Fish Piss* still matters. Just recently I attended the first Halifax Artbook Fair, put on by a group of NSCAD graduates. At one table were two very young women selling their scrappy zines. I approached them to check out their wares. They had come all the way from Montreal for the event. We got to talking about zines and they asked me, "Have you ever heard of a zine called *Fish Piss*?" I doubt they were born when it folded. *Fish Piss* made its own culture, speaking the familiar accent of a Montreal Rastelli so desperately sought in his teen years, expanding the Venn Diagram further afield, eventually influencing others outside its sphere, but also nurturing those within. The fact that *Fish Piss* featured the first publications of award-winning writers, functioning as what Rick Trembles calls "a time-capsule," is enough in itself to secure a legacy.

ARCMTL, originally called Archive Montreal, is a non-profit organization founded in 1998 with a dual mandate to promote and preserve independent culture and has become the umbrella group for many of the activities *Fish Piss* started. The original idea was to archive the "ephemera" of various "scenes" but it has grown significantly to the point where a rented studio space is filled with old publications, posters, flyers, and more. When I visited, Rastelli had just received the entire archive of photographs from the recently defunct alternative weekly the *Montreal Mirror*. I was impressed by the scores of bulging filing cabinets. ARCMTL's archive centre is used by researchers and provides rare materials for use in museum exhibits, publications, compilations of music or spoken-word, documentary films and television series and more. ARCMTL also produces and collaborates on exhibits, oral history projects and conferences year-round, including on-going online projects such as Montreal Underground Origins and Nights of Montreal, where histories and material from Montreal's 1960s and 1970s arts milieu are presented. In recognition of its unique contribution and impressive track record, in 2016 the Conseil des arts de Montréal named ARCMTL a finalist for its annual Grand Prix award.

As mentioned, a group of us got tired of travelling to Toronto for zine fairs and being shut out of the French establishment, so we started one ourselves at La Sala Rossa and called it Expozine. That first year, there were about fifty exhibitors, mostly English. Now in its twentieth year, it features almost three hundred exhibitors, mostly French, with fifteen thousand visitors, making it one of the largest events of its kind. And, of course, the "bohemian" vibe of the festival is often noted. When I was at the London Art Book Fair, AA Bronson of the art group General Idea was commenting on a festival in Montreal that was so much better because it was so very *inclusive,* and I realized he was talking about Expozine. In this sense, Expozine is an example of what Duncombe calls "the celebration of the amateur." As the cultural global network becomes more and more corporate and therefore more "professional," Rastelli is supporting amateurs and all they stand for—the need to express themselves outside the rigid (and often expensive) constraints of the mainstream.

In 2018, ARCMTL launched Volume MTL, the city's first annual fair and conference dedicated entirely to art books. The organization is also a founding partner of the Montreal Printed Art Festival. As part of this festival, ARCMTL organizes the annual GRANDE Print Art Fair, a gathering of more than fifty artists and organizations from Montreal's printmaking and poster art community.

ARCMTL also repurposed obsolete cigarette vending machines into art dispensers to create Distroboto in 2001, has since provided twelve hundred artists with an alternative distribution network to sell more than one hundred thousand items. Rastelli hints at the legacy of *Fish Piss* when he says, "A lot of the artists seemed to appreciate having this direct line to send out a trial balloon." The

Distroboto was even featured in a *New York Times Magazine* "Ideas" issue in 2001. Perhaps the most interesting project for the Distroboto was a collaboration for the Montreal Biennale in 2007. The SBC Gallery of Contemporary Art hosted a Distroboto on the premises for the duration of the show, and Rastelli asked comic artists to make "maps" which folded up into the machines. I made a map with Joe Ollmann called *Milo & Sam* about pushing our toddlers around the Plateau in strollers. The most significant map for the purposes of this book is the one Rastelli made with comic artist Billy Mavreas. It features a map of downtown Montreal with all the venues labelled that Rastelli frequented in his youth, most of which have come and gone. Bohemia needs its venues, even in hindsight. Other artists involved who also contributed to *Fish Piss* were Rupert Bottenberg, Richard Suicide, and Hélène Brosseau.

To come full circle, we can expand Marshall McLuhan's oft-quoted phrase "the medium is the message" with something more, as Duncombe suggests:

> The medium of zines is not just a message to be received, but a model of participatory cultural production and organization to be acted upon. The message you get from zines is that you should not just be getting messages, you should be producing them as well… doing it yourself is the first premise of participatory democracy.

So, the legacy of *Fish Piss*, like so many other zines, is one that sets an example of participatory democracy.

As a society we need Bourdieu's "prestige of romantic triumph," and it was Montreal in the time of *Fish Piss* that perfectly fulfilled this need. As Efrim of Godspeed explains:

> There was some point maybe two years ago before all this shit started, there would be shows in spaces we liked in Montreal where it wasn't great, it wasn't like everything had come true, but there was, like, a glimmer. ... You can't name it—something that would mean that life wasn't shit— but you don't even see that glimmer in the space between the window and the window frame anymore.

What he is describing is a glimmer of hope, and it was venues like Hotel2Tango, before they were discovered by Wire and the mainstream press, that provided that hope.

And it is the vision of Louis Rastelli that created this "big variety true-false mix" that anyone interested in Canadian culture should now revisit. As Mavreas says, "I think *Fish Piss* is more important than we realize. Because Montreal doesn't mythologize itself in the same way as other Canadian cities do, we often lose count of the threads that helped shape not only the local scene but the national one. I think Louis himself has not received the recognition for the work he continues to do, let alone all the work he has already done."

Why does *Fish Piss* matter? It matters because it provided a successful template to an anti-corporate model of culture. It matters because it was emblematic of a contact zone, where a multiplicity of artforms overlapped and created something new, often something that couldn't be defined. It mattered because it traded on its linguistic capital and was as bilingual as its editor, at a time of division and separation. It mattered because it brought people together. It mattered because of the budding artists who saw themselves in the zine, then made more work to contribute, thus producing their own culture, rather than having it dictated to them. It mattered because those artists rubbed metaphorical and physical shoulders with other artists like themselves at spoken-word events and music shows and were able to find their tribe or leave it all behind and move to the suburbs. But it was their decision. They were able to dip their toes into the alternative and not be shut out of their own lives. It mattered because it provided that glimmer of hope before everything changed forever, and in doing so the community around *Fish Piss* exists, in hindsight, as the last authentic bohemia.

But was it all worth it? I will let Rastelli have the last word:

> While the so-called 'alternative' weeklies write almost exclusively about those things that have a dollar sign attached to them, there are still more than enough things worth documenting that provide no financial

incentive for us to write about. That's where people like me come in. I lose money, and I spend a heck of a lot of time on what we do, but the end result will always be worth it.

ACKNOWLEDGEMENTS

For many years I had wanted to write this book, but I just never had the time. I couldn't even imagine myself making a sandwich, let alone writing a *proposal* for this book. Then I saw the Exploded Views series from Coach House Books. I thought maybe that could be the container for my idea, and was encouraged by editor Alana Wilcox to submit something. By the time I was able to actually get it done, the series was defunct. But I thank her for her encouragement.

In the spring of 2020, my family, along with the rest of the world, was in lockdown. We were in our Atlantic bubble. No one got in or out of the province of Nova Scotia and as such, there were zero cases of Covid 19 for the longest time. Our two youngest boys were at the South Shore cottage with their grandmother, and we brought them groceries once a week. Our oldest was pretty much independent, doing his training and online school. So, I had a lot of time on my hands for the first time in decades. I read. I drew. I walked. I thought about reading and drawing while walking. But it was when I realized the two younger boys would be coming back from the cottage in three weeks that it occurred to me that I had a window.

So over twenty-one days straight, fourteen hours a day, in the height of the pandemic lockdown, I wrote this book. I want to thank my children (Angus, Silas, Milo) for staying occupied. And especially I want to acknowledge my wife Christy Ann Conlin for being a solid rock behind the scenes running the house, and for her loving support, but also for her perspective and guidance as an accomplished writer herself. I could not have done it without her.

Thanks to Billy Mavreas for introducing me to so much amazing DIY culture, including of course, *Fish Piss*.

Many of the quotes from Montreal musicians are taken from Geoffrey Stahl's important essay "Tracing out an Anglo Bohemia." This was an invaluable source.

Thanks to Merv Horgan for giving me an outsider perspective.

Thanks to Catherine Kidd and Corey Frost, who are pretty much the smartest people I know, and without whom I would never have become a publisher.

Thanks to all the contributors to *Fish Piss*, especially the comic artists who were such a mind-blowing revelation to my sheltered West Coast upbringing. I am still publishing the work of these talented artists.

Thanks to all the artists who gave us permission to reproduce their art on the *Fish Piss* covers. Special thanks to Caro Caron whose art graces the cover of this book, and to David Drummond who created the final cover.

Since I started writing this book, the Montreal community has lost a number of artists. RIP Henriette Valium,

Geneviève Castrée, Bernie Mireault, and Jake Brown.

Thanks to Meg Sircom for being there.

And of course, thanks to Simon Dardick, Nancy Marrelli, Carmine Starnino, and Willow Loveday Little at Véhicule Press. Simon was an early inspiration for Conundrum Press and was part of an earlier bohemian community in Montreal. Publishers are a rare breed—pragmatic optimists that they are—and they usually don't get enough credit. So, I give credit where it is due.

And finally, I want to thank Louis Rastelli, whose passion and energy for alternative culture is unparalleled. Every arts community deserves a driving force like Louis.

WORKS CONSULTED

Ackerman, Marianne. "Where future greatness gets its break," *Montreal Gazette*, Nov 19, 2007.

Bakewell, Sarah. *At the Existentialist Café* (Vintage, 2016).

Baldick, Robert. *The First Bohemian: The Life of Henry Murger* (Hamish Hamilton, 1961).

Baldwin, James. *Notes of a Native Son* (Beacon Press, 2012).

Beaty, Bart. *Fredric Wertham and the Critique of Mass Culture* (University Press of Mississippi, 2005).

Bigge, Ryan. "Hiding in Delight: Transgression, Irony and the Edge of Vice," Ryerson University, 2007.

Bigge, Ryan. "Searching for Breakfast and Bohemia," *Broken Pencil* #24, 2003.

Bradbury, Malcolm, ed. *The Atlas of Literature* (Prospero Books, 2001).

Braude, Mark. *Kiki Man Ray: Art, Love, and Rivalry in 1920s Paris* (Norton, 2022).

Broken Pencil. Issue #5 (1997), #6 (1998), #7 (1998), #8 (1999), #10 (1999), #12 (2000), #13 (2000), #14 (2000), #24 (2003), #50 (2010).

Brown, Andy. "Fear and Loathing at Bistro 4" *index*, April 1995.

Brown, Andy. "Comix en ville," *Matrix* #56, Montreal *bandes dessinées* issue, 2000).

Brown, Andy and Ollmann, Joe. *Montréal: Comic City*, Distroboto edition (SBC Gallery of Contemporary Art, 2007).

Brown, Andy, ed. *20x20: Twenty Years of Conundrum Press* (Conundrum, 2016).

Brown, Andy, ed. *BDQ: Essays and Interviews on Quebec Comics* (Conundrum, 2017).

Brown, Lauren Alexandria. "A Zine of One's Own: DIY and Alternative Expression among the Beats and the Riot Grrrls," Senior thesis at Union College (2013).

Camlot, Jason and Swift, Todd, eds. *Language Acts: Anglo-Quebec poetry, 1976 to the 21st Century* (Véhicule Press, 2007).

Carpenter, Humphrey. *Geniuses Together: American Writers in Paris in the 1920s* (Unwin Paperbacks, 1987).

Catchlove, Lucinda. "How the Godspeed Generation made Montreal the Center of the Indie Rock Universe," Redbull Music Academy, September 28, 2016.

Cate, Phillip and Shaw, Mary, eds. *The Spirit of Montmartre* (Rutgers University, 1996).

Cook, Bruce. *The Beat Generation: The Tumultuous '50s Movement and its Impact on Today* (William Morrow and Company, 1971).

Costa, Maddy. "Godspeed You! Black Emperor – the full transcript," *The Guardian*, Oct 2012.

Dardick, Simon. Interview, June 19, 2020.

Davey, Frank. *When Tish Happens* (ECW, 2011).

Dell, Floyd. "The Fall of Greenwich Village," 1926. Found in Grana, César, Grana, Marigay, eds. *On Bohemia: The Code of the Self-Exiled* (Transaction Publishers, 1990).

Doucet, Julie. *Dirty Plotte: The Complete Collection #2* (Drawn & Quarterly, 2018).

Duncombe, Stephen. *Notes from Underground: Zines & the Politics of Alternative Culture* (Microcosm, 1997, 2001).

Dunlevy, T'Cha. "Godspeed's Efrim Manuel Menuck sings

from the shadows on solo album," *Montreal Gazette*, Feb2, 2018.
Dylan, Jack, ed. *Park Towers* #6, 2004.

Florida, Richard. *The Rise of the Creative Class* (Basic Books, 2002).
Ford, Hugh. *Published in Paris: American and British Writers, Printers, and Publishers in Paris, 1920-1939* (Garnstone Press, 1975).
Four Minutes to Midnight #12, Expozine Edition, 2011.
Frey, Julia. *Toulouse-Lautrec: A Life* (Viking, 1994).
Fried, Golda. *Nellcott Is My Darling* (Coach House Books, 2005).
Fried, Golda. *Darkness then a blown kiss* (Gutter Press, 1998).
Fried, Golda. *Hartley's Stories* (Conundrum, 1997).
Friedman, R. Seth, ed. *Factsheet 5* #59, 1995. "An interview with Tower's Zine Buyer, Doug Biggert" by Mike Wooldridge, page 10.
Friedman, R. Seth, ed. *Factsheet 5* #63, 1998.

GODBERD. "What Happened to Jack Dylan," https://godberd.com/m/events/view/WHAT-HAPPENED-to-Jack-Dylan?eid=223&pid=0, accessed June 18, 2020.
Goldstein, Jonathan. *Lenny Bruce is Dead* (Coach House Books, 2001).
Goodman, Fred. *Why Lhasa de Sela Matters* (University of Texas Press, 2019).
Grana, César, Grana, Marigay, eds. *On Bohemia: The Code of the Self-Exiled* (Transaction Publishers, 1990).

Hage, Emily. *Dada Magazines: The Making of a Movement* (Bloomsbury, 2023).
Hahn, Emily. *Romantic Rebels: An Informal History of Bohemianism in America* (Houghton Mifflin, 1966).

Hale, Joe. *Love and Forgiveness* (Swimmers Group, 2014).
Hale, Joe. Untitled (Spontaneous Productions, 1999).
Harrington, Michael. "We Few, We Happy Few, We Happy Bohemians: A Memoir of the Culture Before the Counterculture," 1972. Found in Grana, César, Grana, Marigay, eds. *On Bohemia: The Code of the Self-Exiled* (Transaction Publishers, 1990).
Henderson, Stuart. *Making the Scene: Yorkville and Hip Toronto in the 1960s* (University of Toronto Press, 2012).

Johnson, Joyce. *Minor Characters: A Beat Memoir* (Penguin, 1994).

Keating, Cecilia. "Zines Never Die: ARCMTL's Twentieth Anniversary," *Montreal Review of Books*, Fall 2018.
Kalynchuk, Valerie Joy. *All Day Breakfast* (Conundrum, 2001).
Kerouac, Jack. *The Subterraneans* (Ballantine, 1958).
Klosterman, Chuck. *The Nineties* (Penguin, 2022).

Leland, John. *Hip: The History* (Harper Perennial, 2004).
Light, Alison. *Mrs. Woolf and the Servants: An Intimate History of Domestic Life in Bloomsbury* (Bloomsbury Press, 2008).
Ludovico, Alessandro. *Post-Digital Print: The Mutation of Publishing since 1894* (Onomatopee 77, 2012).

Mailer, Norman. "The White Negro," 1957. Found in Grana, César, Grana, Marigay, eds. *On Bohemia: The Code of the Self-Exiled* (Transaction Publishers, 1990).
Martin, Justin. *Rebel Souls: Walt Whitman and America's First Bohemians* (Da Capo Press, 2014).
Mavreas, Billy. *Mutations: The Posters of Billy Mavreas* (Conundrum, 1997).

Mavreas, Billy. Interview by author, April 20, 2017.
McGillis, Ian. "Bohemian Rhapsody," *Montreal Review of Books*, Fall 2007.
McGillis, Ian. "Montreal's Fertile Fields: 20 Years of Literary Landscape" *Montreal Review of Books*, Fall 2017.
McKeen, Graham. "Being Photographed" *index*, March, 1996.

Ngui, Marc. Interview by author, June 1, 2020.
Ngui, Marc. *Enter Avariz* (Conundrum / Bumblenut, 2002).
Ninjalicious. *Access All Areas* (Infiltration Presents, 2005).
Norris, Ken. "How the Tish Poets Came to Influence the Montreal Scene." Barbour, Douglas ed. *Beyond Tish* (West Coast Line, 1991).

O'Neill, Heather. *Two eyes are you sleeping* (DC Books, 1998).
O'Neill, Heather. *Lullabies for Little Criminals* (Harper Perennial, 2006).
Parry, Albert. *Garrets and Pretenders: A History of Bohemianism in America* (Dover, 1933).
Piepmeier, Alison. "Why Zines Matter: Materiality and the Creation of Embodied Community," American Periodicals, 2008, Vol. 18, No. 2 (2008), pp. 213-238. Published by: Ohio State University Press.
Pierrot, Grégory. *Decolonize Hipsters* (Between the Lines, 2021).
Polsky, Ned. *Hustlers, Beats, and Others* (Anchor Books, 1969).

Rastelli, Louis, ed. *Fish Piss*, #1 (1996), #2 (1997), #3 (1997), #4 (Winter/Spring 1998), #5 (1999).
Rastelli, Louis, ed. *Fish Piss*, Vol 2, No 1 (#6, 2000).
Rastelli, Louis, ed. *Fish Piss*, Vol 2, No 2 (#7, Fall/Winter 2002).
Rastelli, Louis, ed. *Fish Piss*, Vol 2, No 3 (#8, 2003).

Rastelli, Louis, ed. *Fish Piss,* Vol 2, No 4 (#9, Fall/Winter 2003/2004).
Rastelli, Louis, ed. *Fish Piss,* Vol 3, No 1 (#10, 2004).
Rastelli, Louis, ed. *Fish Piss*, Special Expozine 10th Anniversary Limited Edition (#11, 2006).
Rastelli, Louis. *A Fine Ending* (Insomniac Press, 2007).
Rastelli, Louis and Mavreas, Billy. *Montréal: Comic City*, Distroboto edition (SBC Gallery of Contemporary Art, 2007).
Rastelli, Louis. *Broken Pencil,* 2012.
Rastelli, Louis. "Fanzines in Quebec, Since 1968," Expozine catalogue (ARCMTL, 2012).
Rastelli, Louis. Interview by author, Jan 31, 2017.
Rosenkranz, Patrick. *Rand Holmes: The Artist Himself* (Fantagraphics, 2010).
Rosset, Barney, ed. *Evergreen Review Reader 1957-1966* (Blue Moon Books, 1993).
Rowe, Chip. *The Book of Zines* (Henry Holt and Co, 1997).
Ryan, Kyle. "Why Punk Planet's Demise Matters," The AV Club Blog, 2007.

Scutts, Joanna. *Hotbed: Bohemian Greenwich Village and the Secret Club that Sparked Modern Feminism* (Seal Press, 2022).
Seigel, Jerrold. "From Bohemia to the Avant-Garde: Dissolving the Boundaries," 1986. Found in Grana, César, Grana, Marigay, eds. *On Bohemia: The Code of the Self-Exiled* (Transaction Publishers, 1990).
Shoumarova, Lina. *Publishing in the Contact Zone: Linguistic properties of the book publishing field in Montreal*, Concordia University, 2007.

Stahl, Geoff. "Tracing Out an Anglo-Bohemia: Music-making and Myth in Montreal" *PUBLIC: Arts, Culture, Ideas*, 2003.

Stanton, Victoria and Tinguely, Vincent. *Impure: Reinventing the Word: The theory, practice, and oral history of 'spoken word' in Montreal* (Conundrum, 2001).
Stover, Laren. *Bohemian Manifesto: A Field Guide to Living on the Edge* (Bulfinch Press, 2004).
Straw, Will. "Scenes and Sensibilities," *PUBLIC: Arts, Culture, Ideas* #22-23, 2001.
Thompson, John B. *Books in the Digital Age* (Polity Press, 2005).
Tousignant, Isa. "Writing on the Wall," *Montreal Hour*, Nov 9-15, 2006.
Trembles, Rick. Interview by author, May 1, 2017.
Trembles, Rick. *Represented Immobilized* (Conundrum Press, 2021).

Verzuh, Ron. *Underground Times* (Deneau, 1989).

Weingarten, Marc. *The Gang That Wouldn't Write Straight* (Three Rivers Press, 2005).
Weintraub, William. *City Unique* (McClelland & Stewart, 1996).
Wetzsteon, Ross. *Republic of Dreams: Greenwich Village: The American Bohemia, 1910-1960* (Simon & Shuster, 2002).
Widgington, David. Interview by author, June 1, 2020.
Widgington, David and Palladino Luca, eds. *Counter Productive* (Cumulus Press, 2002).

INDEX

FISH PISS COVERS PRODUCTION CREDITS

No. 3	Silkscreening by Henriette Valium
No. 4	Front and back colours and silkscreening by Simon Bossé (Mille Putois)
No. 5	Front and back colours by Siris and Line Gamache; silkscreening by Simon Bossé (Mille Putois)
No. 6	Colours by Henriette Valium, Louis Rastelli and Simon Bossé; silkscreening by Simon Bossé (Mille Putois)
No. 7	Colours and silkscreening by Leila Majeri
No. 8	Front and back colours by Uncle Costa; silkscreening by Dominique Pétrin
No. 10	Colours and silkscreening by Séripop (Chloe Lum, Yannick Desranleau)